Mystical

Ronda Robertson

*To my daughter,
for your children and your children's children.
When the heart is in the right place,
we see everything.*

Ever since

Look into your heart, my child
For that is where your future belongs.
You gotta look into your soul
So your spirit can be free.
You taught me this one summer's day
For yours is the new world
With some endless possibilities.
The sun was beating down, when she told me.

Ever since I was a little girl
I held the dream up high,
Held the dream up high.
When a newborn baby greets this world
We hold the dream up high,
Hold the dream up high.

You gotta look into your heart
When you speak,
When you speak.
Child, what you're worth to me
Don't you know it?
Fills my heart with joy.
She held my tiny hand
As we walked across the desert earth.
The sun was beating down
Across the orange earth
Shadows in the dirt.

Ever since I was a little girl
I held the dream up high,
Held the dream up high.
When a newborn baby greets this world
We hold the dream up high,
Hold the dream up high.

Lyrics by Ronda Robertson

Some names have been changed to protect identities.

Testimonials

Erica's experience

My first encounter with Ronda was early in 2013 at an expo. I have had many readings before and never really thought anything of them. After seeing Ronda, I had chills because I couldn't come to terms with how she would know anyone within my family, let alone my ambitions and goals. I saw Ronda again but this time with my twin sister in the room, later in 2013. This passage is a segment on my experience with having a reading done by Ronda.

My experience was different because I couldn't imagine her telling me about people I haven't even met who had died. Having a European background, I couldn't imagine how this lady could possibly pronounce any Serbian names correctly. It was clear that she was talking/seeing the dead and was communicating through them. Ronda was good when it came to giving descriptions of these people who were dead. The messages I got through Ronda were from my grandmother whom I had never met, my grandmother's sister, my cousin who is still alive, my grandpa's friend in Serbia and others who knew my father.

My grandmother seemed to be in a lot of the reading. She was able to describe a decking at the front and back of the house which my father had built in our home. She wanted me to pass the message that she likes it. She came to Australia once, which she told Ronda. She was able to describe where she is now, that it's peaceful, she's living in nature with the birds, trees and animals and loves it. She was describing the memorial park where her ashes were buried. She wanted me to tell my father she loves it where she is now.

My grandmother showed Ronda a baby she was holding and showing her that the baby couldn't breathe. She looked upset and sorry. She mentioned the name of my aunty (my father's sister and the baby's mother). She explained to Ronda that my aunty was going through problems in her life. Ronda told me that my grandmother showed her the baby while explaining through actions that the baby died with something wrapped around his neck. I was stunned because no one knew about this and the baby did die by its own umbilical cord. My grandmother wanted me to pass the message on to my aunty that baby is fine and she is looking after him and she should be proud of herself.

My grandmother described to Ronda that I have a cousin that works with his hands and has his own business. It was weird because my cousin is a chiropractor and works with his hands. Ronda said the name Marko, which is my cousin's name (he's still alive). She was able to point out that he is in his teens, experimenting with alcohol and so on. He is seen as macho but he is a real softy inside. She said that his energy was very strong and stood by me. She explained that he is experiencing some difficulty with something and struggling in terms of his life. This is true because my cousin finished his last exams, is experimenting with life and he has been through a lot of difficulties with his friends and girlfriend.

Ronda was encountered by my grandfather's friend who passed away not long ago. He was my grandfather's friend in the military and grew up with him. She explained John wanted to say hello to him.

Throughout the reading, Ronda described an elderly man in between four walls sitting on a chair with the TV off, tapping his walking stick on the floor every so often. She said all he does is think of my sisters and I and how far we have come and how proud he is. Ronda picked up my grandfather who is alive and lives in a bungalow outside our house. He doesn't socialise and sits with the TV off and taps his walking stick every now and then.

Ronda was able to pick up my first dog who passed away and whom I loved when I was younger.

Laura's testimonial

I don't think I will ever forget my first experience with Ronda. I have been to many psychics before but nothing compared to how accurate Ronda's readings were. At the time I went to see Ronda, I had been in a confused and lost state of mind. I remember just wanting some kind of reassurance to know if everything would be okay. Ronda not only helped provide the reassurance but she was also able to identify things that had happened in my past that no one else knew about. She also was able to identify family members who had passed away by their names. I was blown away at how much she knew about me without me saying a word.

Ronda was able to tell me things about my mother I didn't even know. She saw my mother with birds all over her when she was young. When I asked my mother, she told me that she grew up with birds and was stunned. Ronda described two males, twins. She said that they are watching over me and that they are looking after me. She asked if I had known them – I said no. She asked if anyone in the family had twins – I said no. But when I asked my mum, she started crying. She wondered how Ronda would know that. My mother's mum (my grandmother) had twin boys that died before birth.

My grandmother's sisters kept coming up in my readings, telling Ronda to pass the message to me to say hi and they miss their sister. Another message came from my dad's uncle who passed – my grandfather's brother, Nikola. He said he wishes he could have a glass of wine and beer with a roast. When I told my dad, he was stunned because he said that's what they would do in the village in Serbia.

Another time I saw Ronda and before I even sat down, she was able to pick up someone who had recently passed away. She described the person and that they couldn't breathe. She said for me and my sister to pass the message on to Slavica, my aunty, that everything is okay and thank you for your help. The person Ronda picked up in the reading was my great-grandfather who had died the day before. He died in intensive care and my aunty was always with him, upset and talking to him even though he couldn't talk back because he couldn't breathe independently.

Garnet's testimonial

I first came across Ronda at a psychic expo. I was sceptical but I thought I had nothing to lose. So why not see what she could tell me? And she was able to pick up on things I couldn't believe, things that hadn't been publicised on Facebook and things that my friends hadn't known. She picked up on a list of five characteristics or events that had occurred recently to a man I had been seeing at the time. Her description of him was spot on; for example, the sports he played and liked, his personality traits, his physique. She even described how his old car had randomly stopped/broken down, and how it had left him stranded. I had felt that this was an odd thing for her to pick up on and be so right about. Why? Because I had met this man a few years ago. We had remained friends but with little contact, yet I distinctly remember his car and the stickers he had on it. It wasn't a fancy car, just one that took you from A to B but I remember meeting up with this man a few years later and realising his car had been replaced. It was news to me, and a few days later this psychic sat in front of me and described this car event to me. She described his hobbies, things that she couldn't have known. She went on to say she didn't feel this man would be my partner – this was a short fling. And a few short months later, she was right.

I then went back to see Ronda a few months later and this time she was able to describe my grandfather to me, a man whom I had never met as he had passed away when my father was a boy. She told me to ask my father specific things, like a photo taken when he was a boy – a photo I didn't even know existed. She even picked up on my grandmother – and this is where things get scary – she picked up on a word. A specific word spoken in another language and not just any common language but in Slovene. This is something she could not know prior to the reading – she didn't know my surname or background, let alone how to speak the language. My grandmother had told Ronda the Slovene word for 'wait'. To wait for the man that is my soulmate and to stop stressing about when he will come. To enjoy life. For Ronda to pick up on a word spoken in a totally different language and not a common one like Italian or French really blew my mind!

Asha's testimonial

Ronda is a fantastic medium. I visit her for a reading once or twice a year, and every time she taps into family members. She has told me the correct names of several deceased members of my family, including my father, grandmother and grandfather. She has passed messages on from them to myself in regards to my life and the path I was taking, and helped me with positive messages while dealing with a difficult break-up. She told me that my father is always sitting next to me, watching over my life, which was very comforting.

I have recommended Ronda to all of my closest family and friends, who have also had positive readings and experiences from her, and would never go to any other medium for a reading.

First published in 2020 by Ronda Robertson
Updated 2022, 2023

© Ronda Robertson 2020
The moral rights of the author have been asserted

All rights reserved. Except as permitted under the *Australian Copyright Act 1968* (for example, a fair dealing for the purposes of study, research, criticism or review), no part of this book may be reproduced, stored in a retrieval system, communicated or transmitted in any form or by any means without prior written permission.

All inquiries should be made to the author.

A catalogue entry for this book is available from the National Library of Australia.

ISBN: 978-1-925921-62-5

Project management and text design by Publish Central
Cover design by Peter Reardon
Cover image by fcscafeine

The paper this book is printed on is certified as environmentally friendly.

Disclaimer

The material in this publication is of the nature of general comment only, and does not represent professional advice. It is not intended to provide specific guidance for particular circumstances and it should not be relied on as the basis for any decision to take action or not take action on any matter which it covers. Readers should obtain professional advice where appropriate, before making any such decision. To the maximum extent permitted by law, the author and publisher disclaim all responsibility and liability to any person, arising directly or indirectly from any person taking or not taking action based on the information in this publication.

Contents

Preface	xvii
The early years	1
Going to the chapel	5
Grace and presence	7
Eternal	13
The opening	15
Turning point	17
Two worlds	21
Grandfather angel	25
Oma	27
Without you I feel lost	31
Doves cry	37
Dreams	41
Moving on	45
I dreamed a dream	47
Faith	49
Interpreter	53
Belief	55
If I go to the temple	59
Frequency	63
Dad	65
Keep an open mind	71
Vision	73
Pink	77
The Princess cross	79
Sign of the cross	81
Signs and symbols	85
Butterfly sister	89
Angels	95
Doorway	97
Echo	101

The birthday party	103
Do you see what I see?	105
Do you hear what I hear?	107
Conscious wave	109
Darren's story	111
Ken's story	115
Della's story	117
Time	119
Robert J's story	121
Ben	123
Walk the walk	125
Spirits have a sense of humour	127
Psychic medium and the aura	129
Animals	133
Fine-tuning	135
Psychic senses	137
Clairvoyance	139
Clairaudience	141
Clairsentience	143
Clairallience	145
Clairgustance	147
Claircognisance	149
The connection	151
Meditation	153
A stitch in time	155
Trust	157
Absent healing	159
Guides	161
The power	165
The third eye	167
Contact	169
Watching over us	171
Nurse Roni	173
The road	177
Mentor	181
Divine plan	183

Mystical

Psychic children	185
Ego and the medium	187
Frequently asked questions	191
When the heart's in the right place, we see everything	205
Crossing over	207
Acknowledgements	209

Preface

It was 2015 after a workplace injury, and I was rehabilitating. It was the injury that changed the course of my life, but yet again another monumental change was about to occur. I was on the way to see my mother to drop off some things for her, and had parked the car in a back street. As I got out of the car, I saw a sign in a shop window and seemed to recollect the name. It was a friend of my sister's, Linda W. As it happened, she was outside her business, not far from our family home, and we spoke. I said I would let my sister know that I had bumped into her.

As Linda passed me her card, she asked, 'Are you writing?'

I thought it was such an odd thing to say, as I'd written songs and recorded an album, but that was years ago. 'No, not at the moment,' I said, thinking initially of music.

She said, 'Oh, I remember an essay you wrote in a high school journal called *Mousey*, a fictitious story about a mouse.'

'Oh my God,' I laughed at my fictious story about a mouse that I'd written so long ago. But she read it, and she must have liked it!

She said maybe I should be writing …

We parted ways, and as I got into my car I was kind of dumbfounded. Write? What could I write about these days, I wondered.

I was so stressed with the injury and rehabilitating, medications and surviving, that it was days later that it suddenly dawned on me. Yes, I could write about being a medium, singer, mother, daughter and nurse, as well as life after death, readings and stories of my childhood growing up in a funeral parlour. I'd been doing platform presentations in mediumship so …

There was a journey emerging, with songs connected to the story of lives, loves, sorrow, defeat, illnesses, cures, mystical occurrences, spirit people, visions, betrayal …

There was energy and the soul and the interconnectedness of love and spirit eternal.

Nursing for over a decade had given me a chance to see suffering and death. I witnessed pallitiative care patients on their own personal quest, trying to heal their emotional wounds. I listened to them as they made peace with relatives and friends. I nursed them until the end, offering comfort and grace, combing back their hair, pulling up the blanket to keep them comfortable, attending to the needs of their families. Listening to a father while on night duty; he was devastated knowing that his days were numbered before his death. He would never speak to his son again, and was contemplating the love he had for him and wondering how he would be remembered. Settling a family before administering the last dose of morphine to a beloved mother, letting them know 'it was the last chance to say goodbye to her'. Ringing a son to come in to the hospital as soon as he could, things weren't going so well. Pulling back the curtain of a room where a child lay after a near fatal accident, unable to speak as the suffering was so intense. Ringing a daughter in the middle of the night to let her know her mother had just passed, waiting for her heart to break before putting the phone down. Walking the line between life and death, I saw the suffering as a nurse.

Sometimes these palliative patients spoke about their fear and leaving loved ones behind. I wasn't a pastoral care worker at the time, but I got a sense of it. The mortal ground we all walk; how it can be challenged through illness. Sometimes hearing a patient speak of their trials through pain and suffering imbues wisdom for others to see themselves as witnesses on a bigger journey. The journey back home is one where we are all bound. In a pastoral role, I was able to be a companion and be present in a way that was spiritual. I could recognise in the 'other' that spirituality was a foundation we could share, regardless of faith. A wellspring of nourishment, healing for the soul. The dimension of the whole could be recognised in the spiritual, not just the body and mind that were being prodded and probed to heal. Both nursing and pastoral care had given me a chance to support the patient in their unique journey. We could weave together the human and the divine. Hearing the stories retold with new possibilities, sometimes new futures were perceived and they could transform. Other stories were bittersweet and healing was impossible but they could transcend, with a recognition that they were more than the physical. They could reframe their situation, they could walk with God/Creator/Source in the here and now. They were able to see the divinity within. They were given the opportunity. It was powerful and it had a lasting effect on me.

Mystical

My teachers and colleagues had given me the opportunity to explore my own spirituality. Different and unique. I had experienced the mystical growing up. Normally I wouldn't speak so much about it. There was sensitivity in the hospital placement as a pastoral care practitioner where I was able to express my journey. I learned through sitting in a sacred circle with colleagues as we untangled life, faith, values, emotions, where we unpacked stories of patients we had seen and how that looked in the light of finding deeper meaning. When debriefing with a spiritual supervisor, I could see other angles unexplored in the visits on the ward and more about myself. Where I was moving closer to revelation and where I was running away. My colleagues became the mirror I was unable to look in. Unable at times to see the pain and suffering I had been been through because it hurt too much, they were reflecting it back in a way that was cathartic and shattering enough for me to break through and see grace. I was changed. I recognised that 'I could love people' and help them to see their own wisdom and vulnerability. I had been that 'other' in the room but now I was free to see more. I could see my journey through God's light.

I also felt it was a legacy for my family to have in the written word the experiences of the spiritual so as to pass them on for future generations. I would have appreciated that kind of knowledge myself, had it been available for me.

I also add to the testimony of mediums all over the world. That every medium is unique and that sensitivity and love fuels the ability. I wonder, too, if that is how the spirit world would have it. I also feared that without writing what I had experienced, it would be lost not only for my daughter and generations to follow but also for the world. I'm still learning and understanding myself, the mystical in all things. I felt writing about it would add another account, another layer for those interested to explore. I also felt that it was necessary to offer the story so that those who were evolving as mediums and psychics could experience through my life story the essence of being informed by one's life and letting that play out and bring wisdom and knowledge to the soul in a raw and sometimes broken way.

I have told these stories countless times to friends and aquaintances in order for them to understand and spread the word.

So I begin the story of the journey that you will encounter. It had to be shared. I revisited the moments and wonder, and found joy through the pain and suffering. I had felt that my journey was grinding to a kind of halt, struggling to survive and defend my case as an injured nurse. What I found was that it was just beginning again. Like the phoenix that rises out of the ashes, I would begin at the end and end at the beginning.

The early years

I was five when we moved to the funeral parlour in the country town of Wangaratta. I recall pulling up in the drive of the parlour, my mother in the front with a baby, and myself and my sister along with Nana in the back seat. Initially Mum didn't want to get out of the car. I think she thought it was a dump with 'what am I getting myself into' running through her mind. Yet there we were – this would be my home for six years and some of my fondest memories belong here in this space and time of my life.

I was eight years old when I saw a dead body in a coffin. Of course, I wasn't supposed to. I believe my parents were very protective in regards to the exposure of their children to dead bodies, like any parents would be. They never talked about it much. There were very few cases that they mentioned apart from a murder case. My mother was traumatised by it and still remembers vividly, to this day, laying out the body with care and sensitivity for the family concerned.

On a sunny afternoon my mother had asked me to bring a cup of coffee to Dad in the workshop where he put the coffins together. I recognise now, as a mother myself, it would have been none too easy to raise a family and assist with the running of the parlour. Mum, although psychic too, was a practical woman and the children came first – she had enough on her plate. So there I was, taking the coffee to Dad; I knocked on the door and proceeded to go in. My eyes immediately went to a body in a coffin. It was blue. Even as a child, I knew without having been educated in spiritual matters that there was nothing there that would hurt me. The soul had vacated the body. As I looked almost curiously around the room, it felt kind of fuzzy, and a veil had appeared. It was almost like I was looking and looking for signs of life and all I could see was blue skin wrapped in a very ornate satin material with beads on it. The very room had a presence of its own, an aura of its own but the body was empty. Like a cocoon a butterfly lives in before finally emerging to fly freely through the sky. My hand started shaking and I thought I would drop the cup, so I backed away and went to Mum.

I said something like, 'Mum, I saw a man in there.'

'Oh, don't be scared darling.' And that was about it.

Mum was probably too busy cooking. Looking back, a great majority of our conversations were at the kitchen sink. Although she's alive now as I'm writing this, I have often wondered if I would be fortunate enough to see her when her time comes.

I also remember being scared of burglars, and saying to her, 'Mum I'm scared that burglars will come to rob us.'

She replied, 'No one would want to rob this place so you don't have to worry about that.'

Spaces that people hold have an energy. The energy that we place in our heart can radiate into a room. It makes sense in a practical way, when we think of lovers and the energy they create in a space, how love can fill the area. The room felt different, a sense of something other than the world we live in, a sense of more than the physical. The room also in a way wavered and disappeared as I looked at the body and then it came back into view. I was too young to capture this intellectually and translate exactly how I felt, yet at the same time the room felt different, softer, silence fell like a curtain that is drawn closed and open at the same time. Death was more than someone's time being up, being done; it was a feeling beyond this reality that emerged. A stillness more still than silence. An ending that was not permanent. Death had an intelligence, a non-judgemental, non-discriminative certainty. The soul needed the body to express the soul. The physical was dispensable in a way. It had told the story of the soul. Time was its vehicle to paint its picture. The breath was gone, motionless, no heartbeat, at peace, at one.

The room on this day had a residual energy of the soul that radiated to every corner. The veil that had unfolded in the room of the deceased, the soul that had returned to spirit was everywhere and beyond but it wasn't in his body. As a child, I recall the room had a strange feeling – oh, so very quiet. I gazed at the corpse but it was clearly vacant with nothing moving it. The room was peaceful and I wasn't scared — it was different but I wasn't scared.

Dad had once done a funeral for someone who had been in jail and he told us that the 'powers that be' had said, 'Oh, just put him in any old box.'

Dad decided he would give the guy a decent service and a decent coffin. In those days, and I'm going back to the '60s, spiritual mentors, guides, spiritual churches or respected mediums were not touring in Wangaratta. Far from it — if you had any psychic visions you were probably considered a bit eccentric or psycho, although spirits and guides and visionaries have been endemic to humanity since forever. Mediums were not doing demonstrations anywhere near Wangaratta at the time.

After the funeral that Dad gave the guy from jail, he said he 'could feel someone thanking him, he could feel a sense of gratitude.' I didn't understand it fully at the time but I recognise now it was information that I would glean much later in life and it would be a reference point. The sense that he had of the spirit thanking him was a natural one and his recollection of the energy exchange was like part of nature working through him as he told the story. He was gifting me that information; perhaps subconsciously he knew more than his mind could comprehend. I was grateful he shared that knowledge and was inspired and kind of awestruck at the time. Still I didn't walk around thinking about it. I simply went on to the next moment in life. It was something that dawned on me later really. This was part of the early years, the fabric that I was immersed in.

We shared that same sense of spirituality and sense that 'we go somewhere', the afterlife, all of us, back home after this journey.

Going to the chapel

Dad thought more spiritually but not so much Mum, even though she gave us evidence many times that she was quite psychic and medium-inclined. But like many on this earthly plane, she never gave her ability the sacredness; she was more of a practical woman. She lived in the now and concepts like spirits and soul presence, although not unlikely for her, were not taken seriously. We clashed on this point many times as she believed there was 'something' but she couldn't pin it down. Dad was more open and perhaps burying the deceased was a reminder to him that there was so much more, and to have faith.

Dad was a country boy whose father had died when he was around six years of age from cancer. He ran away from home in his teenage years as he didn't get along with his stepfather and lived with an uncle. He was rebellious and loved to challenge authority and ideals, and was stubborn to the bone. His laughter was infectious and he was theatrical and funny. His temper was what let him down, though. Temperamentally inclined, he could snap in an instant. We clashed on most things yet his love of art and creativity was where we could bond. Because his father had died when he was young, we missed out on the heritage that he would have given us through having a living grandfather. Perhaps if his father had not passed so young, Dad would not have gone off the rails like he did.

Mum's side were Australian and though her father didn't fight in World War II, his brother did and died. She and Nana knitted socks and scarves for the soldiers who were sent to war. Her side went back to the McKenzies of northern Scotland. The family tree was traced by a relative to Castle Kinkell in Gairloch, Highlanders. They sang around the piano and loved playing cards. They lived not too far from the Caulfield Racecourse and Mum's father would take her as a child to watch the horses as they trained in the early hours of the morning. Her two uncles were children's physicians and surgeons, hardworking and dedicated. They donated money to St Andrew's Hospital in Melbourne, now Peter MacCallum.

Nana lived with us for her entire life. She was a cool and calming presence – I believe the psychic/medium ability was passed on from her side. She was known to have dreams that came true, particularly of the Melbourne Cup and which horse would win. She was also a profoundly good judge of character with a discerning and softer energy and a wise womanly presence about her. Her brother died in World War I at Passchendaele, near Ypres in France, where many of the Australian soldiers fought. Her husband passed years before she did. I remember my grandfather as a grounding presence and a hard worker. At least a third of the backyard was a garden lovingly tendered by him and there was an assortment of vegetables growing there, including a passionfruit vine. I called it my secret garden and would sneak in there and play when I was little. Fond memories of my mother and grandmother shelling peas from the garden are instilled into my mind, along with Grandpa's apple tree.

I guess because of Dad's exposure to death, the experience of burying people and the sadness and grief of losing loved ones, he was in another zone for that period of his life on a day to day basis as a funeral director. Because of that exposure, I wonder if both Mum and Dad didn't thank their lucky stars for the family they had given life to, time and time again.

Another moment I should recount is when Dad and I were driving in the car and he stopped to have a break from the drive and have a cigarette. We got out of the car somewhere near Shepparton. It was an overcast day, the landscape flat with scattered gum trees, a stirring wind and some sheep in the distance.

Dad was drawing back on a cigarette and said, 'God's in nature.'

I think I was around 10; the words sunk in deeply as I looked out at the scenery. It's something I still think of today – God's in nature. Was he thinking of someone he had buried, of the families that grieved and of the way a body vacated appeared void of the spark of the divine, void of the miracle of life? Did death speak to Dad? Did it awaken in him a sense of the mystical and wonder of being here on the earthly plane and yet also belonging to our father in heaven?

Grace and presence

We went to the Catholic school, although we weren't Catholic. I remember wanting to be Catholic and loving the stories of Jesus, Mary and Nazareth. This was enlightening and my spiritual antenna seemed to rise to absorb these stories. As a child, I took relics to school from the parlour and relics for birthday presents that I stole from the workshop.

I was the eldest girl of what was to be six girls and the dead were dressed in really fabulous outfits, bedazzled gear that was too good to be left packaged in boxes in the workshop where Dad put the coffins together. So my sister closest in age and I dressed in them one afternoon. We put on long flowing white satin robes with beaded embroidery on them, pretending to be fairies and angels singing and splashing around in the backyard, which was grassy and muddy.

Then we were found by Dad. 'Get out of those! I have to bury someone in one of them tomorrow!'

Oops.

We had the chapel in the front section of the house where we lived. This was for the funerals, which we were not allowed to go to; this was a sacred space and was off-bounds. But as if we took notice of that! In our innocence, we played there when Dad was preparing for the funerals and Mum was busy with babies. My other sister and I stood at the pulpit singing *Stop in the name of love* and all the cats and teddy bears and empty chapel pews heard our voices rise.

One day Dad had just finished a funeral and he came in laughing so much tears were rolling down his cheeks. 'Who messed with the music tapes?' he asked as we were sitting on the couch.

I knew it wasn't me, but I strongly suspected my younger sisters who had got into the act of playing in the chapel. Instead of the hymn *Abide with thee* as the first song for the service *Zip-a-dee-doo-dah* had played instead. OMG. Crikey, we all laughed out, very loudly.

I think as a child I was attracted to religion and was mesmerised by the statues of Mary at primary school. I would pray with rosary beads in the church at times after and before school. I had visions of becoming a nun before knowing what that really meant. I would wander through the chapel at home when there was no one in it, loving the sense of sacred space, smelling the air, envisaging the congregations that had been there and taking it all in. I believe I wasn't at that point in time sensing Spirit but there was a sense of the creator/the All/God in the chapel, and in those walls I could sense the divine. I could sense a kind of deliverance to spirit and the resonance that the walls shared. We were often told to be quiet while a service was on and indeed we were. There were many times I could hear crying and the grief of those who were lamenting a loved one. Alone in the chapel, I would walk between the pews and linger in what seemed like the thoughts of those who had graced them. It was as if I were being watched at times by Spirit divine. It was sacred ground and it felt that way.

Many years later, a colleague who did a reading for me said that Spirit had been waiting to work with me since I was a little girl.

I was christened Church of England/Anglican but went to the Catholic primary school in Wangaratta. I'm christened Anglican but in my heart I'm open faith. I learnt much from the Catholic tradition and align with the concept that the soul returns to Spirit.

We were the only Anglican children at the school at the time. I loved the stories about Jesus, God and the visions that people had of angels, as well as the Christian ethics. I was in the choir and the music that we sang was beautiful. We came third at the community centre concert where Mum and Dad faithfully sat through the recital of *Joseph and the Amazing Technicolour Dreamcoat*. Our harmonies were exquisite.

The themes of music and spirituality were a central part of my life, the music especially so. My mentor was Shirley Temple. I was four when I asked my grandmother to put my hair in ringlets and rehearsed a song with small rocks that I stuck to the soles of my shoes. I tapped as best I could.

Mystical

'Do I sound like Shirley Temple?' I asked my grandmother.

She replied, 'Yes, dear,' as she looked up from her knitting.

I thought that was a pretty lame answer at the time, but looking back, it's one of my fondest memories. The humility she offered, her service to the family and gentle kindness I carry with me today.

I reflect back on moments like that, especially singing in the chapel. The feeling was free and unencumbered, like coming home somehow and now knowing that in sensing the spirituality in myself I could be a light for others. As a young child, I had dreams of flying and would love those dreams.

We didn't have money; far from it. I had a bike when I was around nine and that was a big deal. One of my younger sisters, who was too little to ride a bike, was a bit peeved so she used the coffin trolleys to scoot around. I have a photo in my collection of her doing this. I remember the children's coffins were white. Dad must have left a coffin open one day as it was on the floor in the workshop and, since he wasn't there, I hopped in it. I had no idea what it was used for, the sorrow of such immensity was beyond my grasp as a child.

We never had some of the things that kids have today – computers, iPads, plasma screens, Xbox, computer games, iPhones, modern toys and talking books weren't around but we had each other.

I was the eldest and so in those early years I would spend time with Dad just hanging out and asking questions while he worked putting the coffins together. Probably one of my most spiritual moments as a child was when Mum had asked him to take me with him as he visited a grave. I sat in the back seat as we travelled on the road to the cemetery. North-eastern Victoria is so beautiful and on this particular afternoon it was no less so. The sky was a dusky pink and orange, and the trees were so tall I couldn't see the tops of them from the car window. I was neatly dressed in a pink and white dress and Dad held my hand as we walked through the cemetery and we came to the grave, freshly dug. I remember Dad shaking the hand of the grave digger so graciously. Yes it was ready, the ground was ready for the burial, I naively had no idea why but 'it was ready'.

One of my sisters had asked Dad as he was busy nailing the coffin together in the workshop, 'Who takes the screws out when they get to heaven?' We laughed out loud and he nearly swallowed the next nail he had ready in his lip to hammer in.

As mediums, we are acting like a conduit for those in spirit to communicate with those who are living. I've learnt to trust and have faith in the messages I'm given and to pass them on but also I strive for a continuing grace in daily life.

Mum had a near death experience; she haemorrhaged after my birth. She states that she travelled to a white light, the brightest white imaginable, and a tunnel in which she was immersed that led to a garden and that the peace she felt was like nothing she could describe on this earth. She says that she heard voices asking her if she wanted to stay there and she remembers saying out loud, 'No, I've just had a baby and I want to return.' And return she did.

After Mum's father passed she also stated that she saw him standing next to the bed she and Dad shared a week after his death. She woke up and saw a vision of him.

She said, 'He looked like an angel, all in white standing next to me and as I reached out to touch him, he disappeared.'

My grandfather, Bill, has made his presence felt since. He visited during a meditation along with a sister who had passed. During the meditation, I saw both he and my sister showing me scissors cutting through material in medieval times. As I came to, I thought, goodness, I was a dressmaker in medieval times. I then realised the image of the scissors meant the scissors cutting through the skin. In other words, I was given a sign that surgery was on the horizon before I actually knew I would indeed have surgery, three months after the vision in meditation.

Some people of a spiritual nature have said that we travel in this lifetime with family that can help us evolve spiritually; that this is part of our soul family and that we choose the mother and father while in Spirit. I am grateful for the family I was born into and I hope that I have been able to help them evolve as well, even though we've had our moments.

The concept of the deceased looking after the living is as old as time itself. It's difficult for many to comprehend as we are so fixed on the material world and the physical body. To step outside of the body and feel, to be aware of the auric field and sensitive to the world of a realm that is beyond can be daunting to many, to say the least, and hocus pocus to others. While with some it's quite natural and part of nature, just as some trees lose their leaves and others keep them.

Mystical

We left the funeral parlour when I was 11 – that meant we left the countryside of northern Victoria with its lush scenery and the hot baked bread we would acquire on a Sunday drive. It also meant I was leaving a primary school, St Patrick's, that I loved, a choir that was magnificent, and the nuns who had taught music, art and history with a passion. My foundations. Dad had gone broke – he was never any good with money, as I learned later on. So it was back to the city with its concrete hills, as I called them. We had occasionally been to the city to my mother's family house, which had a piano. I had travelled there and back many times previously and, upon returning each time, I used to draw a keyboard on a concrete slab with chalk and then pretend to play. Life was changing, taking a twist and turn directly towards Melbourne.

Eternal

The city was a harsh contrast to country Victoria but we now lived in a beautiful Victorian house in East Malvern that had been handed down to Mum through her family. Mum was born in the house and had her tonsils out there as well. This amazing Victorian bungalow had incredibly high ceilings with rosettes on them and chandeliers hanging in two of the main rooms. There was a glorious light that would stream in through the front room, which had four beds in it. There was a mural on one of the walls that was in the entrance hallway and we got many comments about it – one of Dad's cohorts painted it as a trade-in for a car. My grandmother and I shared another room. We had fireplaces in the two front bedrooms that were boarded up. The piano was in one of two rooms that could have served as a dining room but never did.

The backyard had a view of the church with its stained glass windows. We would hear the bells ringing at 7am and 11am on a Sunday morning for service, though Mum and Dad rarely attended even though they were Christian. This was the '70s. It was a middle-class area and, although the house was on a normal size block, it was one of the oldest in the street.

Dad went to work as a used-car salesman. We got through. I think he struggled with the transition and the work was more superficial. There was a sense of lingering and things seemed to travel faster in the city. He would at times bring home clothes that people had given him generously for the family. I think he struggled financially and didn't know what to make of things.

At our new school, the children swore (something we would not consider at the Catholic school). There was no choir at the primary school and little talk of religion. I didn't have to wear a uniform or blazer. My good friend Caroline took me under her wing and a new life began. I still maintain a friendship with a couple of the girls I met in primary school.

The pace was different and it felt as if I were caught up in some vacuous tunnel. Life was changing. Looking back now, I think I missed the presence and grace of the chapel, the environment of going there and walking through the pews where people sat. I didn't feel anchored when we moved back to the city for a while. It was a period of transition, looking back. I felt comfortable in the country and that environment. I preferred the quietness of simply walking around the chapel on my own. But life changes and as I got to know new friends and started to ease into the new, things merged in their own way.

I was never brilliant at maths and by the time we moved I had missed out on quite a chunk of the theory. The grade was moving on and I fell behind. I coped well with other subjects but missing out on maths was a hardship that took ages to catch up on. The city was faster and it took a while to get used to the pace.

The opening

It was when I was 14 that my thoughts on the afterlife changed forevermore. There was a funeral that my parents had attended; we as children hadn't gone. Upon returning, Dad, as usual, was in the room where as a family we sat and watched TV. He had a comfortable chair that he was reclining in and my sister was sitting in another chair and I was on the couch. Dad poured a beer from a can into a glass, put them back on the coffee table and as he sat back in his chair the beer can slowly elevated, succinctly and miraculously, approximately 8 to 10 inches into the air and approximately six inches across before descending back slowly down onto the table. Where it landed. Our jaws dropped as we silently gazed from the beer can mid-air to each other. It wasn't a quick occurrence – it lasted about 16 seconds. We weren't scared – there was complete silence and peace emanating within the room and we subconsciously knew it had something to do with the passing as it was the afternoon of the funeral. It was a miracle. Numinous, a mystical experience.

After the can had landed back on the table, half a minute later, Mum walked into the room. What timing!

Dad said, 'Audrey, you won't believe what just happened. The beer can moved on its own.'

'Closer to you, I suppose,' she replied.

With that, we all just laughed as we knew it was beyond amazing and that you had to be there. Seeing is believing.

But it happened and it's my story, my truth, for the world to hear – a revelation, an opening of wonder, a mystical occurrence, brilliant, giving an insight into the universe where we all belong.

My sister and I have spoken about it since and she has testified that it happened while in the company of her son and his fiancé. We witnessed the 'numinous', a phrase coined by Rudolph Otto, a German Lutheran theologian, philosopher and comparative religionist. Numinous means that the idea of the holy contains more than moral and ethical elements.

Later, in my studies of pastoral care, religion and philosophy, I found Rudolph Otto and his thinking on the numinous ...

> A characteristic common to all types of Mysticism is the identification, in different degrees of completeness, of the personal self with the transcendent Reality. This identification has a source of its own, with which we here are not concerned and which springs from 'moments' of religious experience which would require separate treatment. 'Identification' alone, however is not enough for 'Mysticism'; it must be Identification with the Something that is at once absolutely supreme in power and reality and wholly non-rational. And it is among the mystics that we most encounter this element of religious consciousness.[1]

We witnessed divine power. It changed my life forever. How could it not have ...

I have since heard other stories of water running from taps that just turn on after people pass. What amazing energy we humans have and are surrounded by. If only we could always use that energy in the most constructive of ways and to the betterment of the human race for one and all. Still, I didn't talk about this to even my most trusted friends. I'm not sure if I thought it was something that might have happened to some people but it had an everlasting imprint on my soul. It gave me hope and a kind of philosophical outlook on the world. Perhaps I thought my friends might think it was just too crazy to believe. I have since heard of many occasions of physical mediumship – this was an example. It gave me a new perspective and many times since then when life has thrown me a curve ball, I have thought about it. That we are more than the material world, so much more than we realise and perhaps will never be able to fully comprehend or analyse because the sacred holds something beyond our understanding. Will the world listen more profoundly to the mystical, to wisdom? I see it every day in children and their bliss.

---

1   Otto, R, *The idea of the holy*, London, Oxford University Press, 1923, p. 22

Turning point

Just to give you a glimpse of the times in the '70s at high school, we were saucy, the hormones kicked in and life was about friends, fun, the beach, hanging out, school, boys and music. *The Brady Bunch* was on TV and *Lost in Space* was a familiar favourite. Stevie Wright was on the radio singing 'Evie let your hair hang down'. I learned how to play pool at 15 and we went to discos well before we were allowed to.

We were the children who witnessed man walking on the moon via a black and white TV. We listened to vinyl records and had to physically move the needle to skip to different tracks before the onset of tapes and then CDs and apps.

Global warming wasn't heard of as we sunbathed at Seaford Beach during the long and consistent summers, followed by autumn and a freezing winter. The boys who liked us and wanted to take us out had to ask for our landline phone number. There was no Facebook or social media and we studied university degrees for free.

We would see the world change in ways that we could never have conceived – new technological advances in electrical engineering, medical treatments and new drugs treating cancers. Biological warfare, computer viruses, robots on mars and the pollution of our world and seas, along with wars and human trafficking, to name a few.

I wanted to be a singer but I hadn't told anyone that's what I wanted to do. I was conscientious at school and had a plan B. I had a natural flair for art and won an art competition at 16 at the local town hall in my age group for a painting I nearly threw away. I folded it in half and the teacher had a fit and unfolded it to enter it in the show. Clearly, I was surprised at the win.

My friend Caroline's brother and his best friend used to ride their bikes past the school and flirt with us at morning recess.

I worked part-time at a food chain as soon as I was old enough to work and met new friends there that I still adore to this very day.

I worked there through high school, literally beginning to work when I was 14 years and nine months old. It was after a shift one night, after 10pm, that I was driving home when suddenly I sensed that something just wasn't right. I thought there was a man lying in the back seat of my car. It was a flash, a vision and at the same time I saw this, I felt it also. Initially I thought that I hadn't closed the door and someone had crept in. I was scared as I was so sure someone was there.

I didn't know what to do whether to keep driving or stop the car, I was wondering how best I would survive. So I pulled over and stopped the car, then I turned around with trepidation very, very slowly to find no one in the back seat. My heart was racing. I actually got out of the car to double-check as the feeling was so intense. I was relieved but confused to find the seat empty. When I got home that night, I said to my mother that something had happened. She thought nothing much of the comment so I went to bed.

The next morning, when I woke I heard Mum on the phone saying, 'I will get Ronda for you.'

Mum gave me the phone. 'It's Eva.'

Eva told me, 'My father died last night.'

My heart sank into the gut of my stomach. 'Oh, I'm so sorry.'

Eva said, 'They thought he had died in the back seat of the car; that's where he was found.'

I asked her, about what time?

'Around 10.30pm.'

I was 19 and I remember thinking, this is not a coincident. I knew it was a powerful event from a psychic mediumistic angle but my heart was breaking for my friend and her mother and family. I never told them about it until years later when her mother said I was like the gypsies of Poland.

Mystical

I have since recounted this story many times in an effort to educate people on the power of the afterlife. It's also not an uncommon occurrence for a medium to be jolted into activity by something that will be enough to make you say to yourself – that's beyond the physical material world that I'm used to living in. I've learnt since then that sometimes people are not ready to be connected with the spirit of their loved ones straightaway. It's important to be sensitive. This incident, like the beer can moving, was another pivotal moment in my life. I was speechless then but I connected the dots. There must be something more than life on earth – there is life after death, a world beyond. The body turns to dust but the soul might be everlasting.

Two worlds

I was passionate about music and singing after high school and although fortunate enough to be selected for teachers' college, I deferred after the first year. I auditioned for bands while studying singing and joined an original band that was Paul Kelly's support act. It was great and I'm grateful for those days. We rehearsed sometimes four nights a week and had the set down pat. One of our songs was played on Triple R radio station. I was around 20 at the time but had no idea of what that really meant.

I lived in a share house with friends. The day I moved in, I thought there was a ghost/presence in the house. My friends thought I was overly dramatic and had a colourful imagination. One night we had a few friends stay over and my sister stayed over as well. She and I slept in the same room that night and we both felt a presence touch us separately on the back. When I felt it, I turned over onto my back, lying there scared and wondering what the hell had just touched me.

Then my sister woke, saying, 'Something just touched me on the back, was it you?'

I said no, and that the same thing had just happened to me. We jumped out of the bed, not knowing what to do or who to call upon. I would know better now, and not be so frightened. We couldn't sleep and were awake all night, and everyone else in the house woke up, too. This was the early hours of the morning. We were all petrified.

Once we experienced this event and were kept up all night, this energy dissipated and we never experienced it in the house anymore. Yet we both definitely felt a touch on the back.

There is a principle in spiritualism that it is the power of love that forms the basis of communication. A medium needs to be present for that. Perhaps because my sister and I were both sensitive, we were picking up on someone wishing to come through or even we were picking up on an energy of someone who had lived in the house.

A similar thing happened another night many years later when my daughter and I were living together. She was 15. She felt a presence in her room that woke her in the middle of the night and she felt so scared.

She told it to 'go to my mother.'

Exactly after she asked the presence to go to my room, she heard me scream out. At that moment, her heart hit the ceiling.

I woke up in the other room, not knowing about my daughter's experience at the time and could sense someone there.

I sat up in bed and spoke to the presence. 'You have died and it's okay to go to where you need to be. It's okay to say goodbye to those you loved.'

I felt it was a boy who had passed over in a car accident. I sensed his mother would be so sad in the next few hours. The feeling was that the presence was male in nature and that he was shocked that it had all happened so quickly. I could feel the shock and sadness and, although feeling this, I was also aware of the wonder of the next realm. I didn't understand at the time but I must have been awake speaking to him and reassuring him that it was alright, he would be guided safely. There was the sense of another world that he was in and I experienced a calmness within me and suddenly wasn't afraid any more. The feeling in the room lingered and within an hour or so, the feeling of the presence totally subsided, giving way to a settling like after a deluge of rain has fallen and a freshness is sensed.

It was a moment when I felt I had conquered a fear, but more than this, a moment where I had experienced a doorway between two worlds and one where I must have grace and compassion. This presence had a body just like I have one now. I was talking to him as if he were right there, as if I were having a conversation with anyone. There was no way that I could prove what I was feeling and why I had suddenly just woken. I also had no idea at the time that my daughter had experienced sensing spirit as well.

When we got up that morning, my daughter said, 'Mum, I felt

something come into my room last night and I told it to go to you. After I did that, I heard you yell out and I was so scared I felt my heart jump out of my skin.'

I was shocked. Did she really say that because I was up in the wee hours of the night talking to a spirit?

I told her about the boy and what I felt had happened to him. She and I both hold this as a special memory we have of Spirit and she was able to move forward without fear and to evolve spiritually after that night. I believe it was an opening of her abilities – she was picking up on the spirit world. We were both humbled by the experience knowing that the spirit world look after their own. We were given a glimpse between the worlds that deepened our connection and sensitivity.

As a medium, it is possible to connect whenever we are open to the world of Spirit, whenever and wherever we may be. Call it a double link if you like, where two mediums can link into the same soul at the same time.

There is a lot of fear out in the community based on religious and cultural ideas that permeate. There can be a more rational approach that the spirit world isn't 'evil'. It has an intelligence. The spirit world is like a room wihin rooms and especially now with mediumistic work, readings and platform demonstrations, you can feel the spirit world around and within us. Like heaven on earth, earth in heaven in some parts.

I'm not the only psychic medium in my family – some of my sisters are, too. My sister and I both dreamed the same dream one night. This isn't uncommon but in this dream we dreamt a girl was raped on the same night. We found out later a girl was raped at the corner of her street on the night we both dreamt it.

We were both overcome with emotion that we had dreamed the same violent dream. At moments like this, as a medium, as a person, you wish you could change things. We hung our heads in silence. We didn't know her but we both wished the best for this girl who had experienced such a horror. Sometimes as a medium you will pick up on these occurrences. My sister and I met on common ground and it strengthened the bond we have for each other, and it also reinforced our ability to trust our gut instincts.

Grandfather angel

It was the 90s and my daughter and I were living in a share household. As fate would have it, a friend of a friend was just separating from her boyfriend and so we decided to share a house. A month or so later, my sister, also now newly single, decided to move in as well. We became a 'tour de force' and a cosy little sub-family of our own, sharing laughter, history, wine, late nights and secret women's business. It was a beautiful house in a leafy suburb and a transition period for all of us.

Shortly after my younger sister moved in, we were looking for a boarder as another friend had just moved out. Unfortunately for me, in those days life was quite turbulent and as a single mother I struggled. The search for the boarder was on and we were keen to instil the household with a fresh new energy and looked forward to interviewing potential new people for that opportunity.

One weeknight, the phone rang and my friend answered it. Thankfully, she didn't give out any information but handed the call to me. I'm truly grateful to this day she had the sense and respect to hand the phone over. Perhaps she was also guided?

It's hard to remember the name the male caller gave but I will never forget the numbness, stasis and as if someone were entering my body from outside of me. I recall a quick vision of a haze behind me and envisioned my grandfather standing there, coming so close to me.

With that, my voice changed as if it were not even my voice speaking. 'It's been taken.'

Then I looked at my hand. It was quite high in the air, much higher than I would ever have held it when holding a phone, and with that the phone receiver was placed onto the cradle.

The room had not been taken.

I didn't think anything much of it until a couple of weeks later when I discovered there was a high-profile murder case. Two two females had an advertisement in the same newspaper as we did and they were looking for a housemate. The murderer had rung them and arranged to meet. He bound, gagged and covered the heads of the three occupants in different areas of the house and shot them at close range.

The homicide squad rang us as those who were murdered had an ad looking for a boarder just as we did at the same time in the same newspaper. The homicide detective asked me if I had received any suspicious calls. I said, 'Yes, there was one guy.' Although I didn't think of the vision at the time, only that he sounded strange to begin with. The detective said we were very lucky. Two females and a male were murdered.

It was as if time had stopped. I could see a vision of my grandfather who seemed to have entered my aura, spoke for me and guided me to put the phone down. I simply told the male caller after hearing him speak, 'It's been taken.'

The vision of my grandfather was strong and the sensation around me seemed hazy, as if I were in another world for a short space in time, as I noticed my hand move in an unfamiliar, slow and determined way to place the receiver down.

I can't say why some have to pass in such an unbearable way as the way these three innocent victims did. My guardian angel was around – I believe it was my grandfather, or the spirit world were clever enough to give the imprint of him to me. My heart shatters just thinking about it. We were in such a similar situation as the household where the tragedy occurred. To this day, I still think about it and the families of those slain.

My head hangs as I write this humbly with tears. May their souls be lifted by love, may their families find peace and comfort in the thought that they will meet again in another time and space, where their hearts will be reunited, free of the pain and suffering, only to know joy once more in the arms of their long-lost beloved.

It was the last time I doubted.

Oma

My mother-in-law lived in Austria through World War II. She remembers being in labour with her first child when bombs were dropping and hearing them as the pains of birth came. She and her husband came to Australia on a ship as migrants with suitcases and made a new life for themselves.

I separated from Oma's son when my daughter was around 18 months old but we kept in contact as I thought it was important for my child to know the history and culture of her father's side. She would also look after my daughter for me when I was working singing; she was very supportive. She had grace and was not judgemental with my decision to leave her son. She truly loved my daughter and we would sit literally for hours hearing about her life in war-torn Austria and the devastation and frustrations of living through World War II. She loved the garden and crocheting, and grew chamomile in her garden along with luscious roses and pumpkins. Quite often when we went to visit, she would have things that she had kept for us from the op-shop. She was charitable and hard-working, and her garden was the envy of many.

Oma had lost a child in his teens to leukaemia, and not long afterwards she lost her husband. She had suffered in her lifetime but had kept a humility about her. She never complained – she had a strength about her and the kind of wisdom in her words and gestures gleaned from trauma. She was loving to be around but also grounded with a sense of the practical. We kept up the contact as it felt like a natural thing and conversed with laughter and joy. I kept a subtle eye on her during the years. Oma always wanted to be a nurse but her parents preferred that she become a seamstress and so, being meek, she did so. When they fell ill, she tended to them as an only child. There was no one else to help her.

She had a gorgeous German accent, a feisty independence and a great sense of humour. Some said she had a resemblance to Ingrid Bergman. We adored her, and I believe that resonated in our visits.

Christmas time for Oma was important as she had specifically brought nativity items from Austria over on the ship. She dressed the tree and sang hymns on Christmas Eve. Being the thrifty, savvy Grandma that she was, she would re-gift and we would always have a bit of a laugh with her ingenuity when it came to saving.

Oma was in her eighties when she passed. She had left a message on the answering machine for my daughter to call her the day before we heard that she had suffered a stroke. I was working in the hospital that she was admitted to, so my daughter and I went to the ward as soon as we could.

The stroke had affected the language centre of the brain, like strokes often do. She was lying vulnerably on the bed but recognised us as we slowly stepped into the room. She had reverted to speaking in German and I had no idea what she was saying but my daughter worked it out. It was to do with love. My daughter recognised the word.

We were silent and felt so small and humble with the beauty of the thought of love on her deathbed. When my daughter's eyes and mine locked with each other, we both felt as if we were transported to another reality knowing that she was so unwell.

We left the hospital feeling as if we had been in an emotional tumbledryer, unable to speak as the tears flowed and memories rushed to fill our minds of times we had spent together with her.

It wasn't apparent to us at that stage whether Oma would survive the stroke and linger.

When we got home, my daughter was the first to notice that two of our light fittings were on the floor and a third one was on a bed, fallen straight down as the light fitting was situated directly over it.

The globes were still in place but the fittings, which were white and round had come off. This had never happened before nor has it happened since. We checked with neighbours the next day – there was no electricity outage.

We were speechless, and as silence seeped into us we both felt that this occurrence had something to do with my mother-in-law. The timing was odd and the presence that we felt in the house seemed to speak of her leaving this world for the next.

I said to my daughter, 'I don't think she will get through this. I feel this is a sign, darling, that Oma is leaving soon.'

I didn't have to say that to my daughter, though, and as I looked at her, she and I both knew somewhere deep in our hearts that this was a sign.

Of course, we weren't there when the light fittings came off but we were there at the hospital that night witnessing the love Oma had for us on her deathbed. She passed three weeks later.

To this day, this occurrence has no explanation but I've included it as part of the mystical in my life. It was the one story my daughter wanted to have as part of the memories in reverence to her grandmother and her life.

My daughter's second pregnancy was tougher than her first. At one point, her partner was unwell and she stayed with her in-laws for nearly two weeks. She had developed gestational diabetes and because of a lack of immunity to a particular disease, she had to be given a blood product at the hospital. She was beside herself.

I was finishing the edit for this book and things were quite intense. My focus has always been on her and so, as a mother, I couldn't help but absorb all the fear and sensitivity building up in her as she bravely kept it together. We managed week by week and her in-laws were so supportive during this time. The love and care they offered goes beyond human words as we all felt the stirring of new life within her.

After a couple of weeks, things settled and we were all relieved as life went on again. I dreamt I saw Oma in a shopping centre about a week later – her face unmistakeably recognisable. She was in a crowd of people, wearing a long coat as I envisioned her. We communicated telepathically and I knew what she wanted – to say hello to her granddaughter, my daughter and 'that everything would be alright'.

When I awoke, I felt I was already awake, as talking to her in the dream was so real. Her timing was perfect. Another pertinent factor when spirits come through in dreams is that it's not unusual that you would feel as if you were awake during the dream. The sensation is so strong as we are communicating with them. This sense of feeling also tells us that it's not like a normal dream. Something spiritual has taken place.

The timing was beautiful and when I rang my daughter to tell her, she was so thrilled and a sense of calm was instilled. We had sent a thought out, like many others do when times are tough and we feel that we need help, a sign, a signal. Some prayers were answered for us.

Without you I feel lost

I'm backtracking for a moment – I'm going back to the year of heartbreak. My daughter was in primary school and my partner had decided it was time for goodbye. He had returned from Europe where he had travelled with an entertainer and I suppose he wanted to move on. He was talented and we were 'holding him back'. I'd never been so heartbroken. Looking back, it was embarrassing how much I cried and, since then, I've been told by friends it took me ages to get over him.

I had been married when I was in my twenties and had my daughter when I was quite young. Inevitably, I separated from the father of my child and met Mark, whom I considered to be my soulmate. We were together for some years. We thought alike and had telepathy between us, which I know isn't uncommon for partners. We were cut from the same cloth. He was super talented as a piano player and was in much demand around Melbourne at the time. His younger brother was also very talented and won a competition that took him to New York to study. Mark was charismatic, and when he played piano it was effortless and the sound was like a kaleidoscope of colours rushing through a prism of water descending from the sky. It was magnificent. Music was everywhere for us and we were participants to this mighty healer. We were a happy and contented family. I met him when I was hired to sing at a wedding and was speechless when I saw him, his eyes, pale blue like the sky, almost as if there might be a bird about to fly across them. We did a few gigs together, got each other's contact details. It wasn't long before we started seeing each other. I felt like a princess standing next to him as he was very much a leader, and switched on when it came to the business of music. I had found my match.

He was endlessly working and rehearsing so at one point my daughter and I were able to travel and stay at an uptown hotel in Adelaide for a week, being spoilt by hotel staff while he did a short tour there. He was waiting at the train station in Adelaide when we arrived early in the morning and he took us back to the hotel where he had a residency. After settling in, he presented me with a small box. He stood there waiting while I slowly opened it. Inside was a beautiful ruby and diamond ring. I took a sharp breath in when I saw it. He put in on my finger. It was slightly too big so I wore it on the middle finger, until it was re-sized. We kissed. Apart from the birth of my daughter, I don't think I'd ever been so happy.

Life was blissful and I learned so much from his calm disposition and confidence as music surrounded both myself and my daughter. I worked at a theatre restaurant after sealing a gig after an audition. Through Mark, I met some wonderful musicians and singers and felt as if I'd finally found my tribe. I belonged and was growing and maturing as an artist in my own right. I continued to intuitively hear music and recorded when I could afford to do so.

Mark had studied at the College of the Arts, which now has the facility for singers to study jazz. That faculty didn't exist in my day so it forced a lot of singers onto the street, using nounce to work it out. He had friends who he had studied with and a network that he had accumulated by the time he had received his degree.

They say love is blind. One day, an artist whose song was playing on the radio rang. I didn't know initially who it was when she rang to speak to him, but as soon as I heard her say her name my heart pounded, though at the time I wasn't sure why. She asked if she could speak with him and so I called him to the phone.

As I left the room I could hear his voice had changed in tone and sounded quite curt, normally not the way he would address a caller on the phone. I heard him say, 'I told you not to ring here.'

The coin dropped immediately. This was in the era before mobiles.

A few weeks later, I asked him straight-out, 'Are you having an affair?'

He said no. I believed him but there was something that just didn't sit right.

As fate would have it, soon afterwards my younger sister called me around 1.30am. She'd been drinking and was slurring her words.

She sounded angry with me when she said, 'What are you doing?'
I didn't understand.

'What are you doing? He's out with someone else. I just saw him at a nightclub with another girl and he left there with her.' It was the woman I spoke with on the phone.

He maintained his innocence, which I found out later was a lie. We continued to be together, though my heart had a serious ridge in it. I think subconsciously I knew but didn't want to admit it.

A few months later, another entertainer thought it might be a good idea for him to go overseas with her and another musician. They went overseas. It was the turning point, the fork in the road.

When he came back, he left us within three weeks. I felt the sting of betrayal and mistrust. This was the heartbreak of a lifetime. We were abandoned and he left us without anywhere to live. A girlfriend moved in with us and life changed dramatically. I felt that I would have a breakdown but kept it together because of my daughter. We struggled. I sold furniture to pay the rent. I pawned my ring at a shop in Chapel Street, as well as musical instruments, anything to keep us alive. Although I sang, I found it difficult to survive just on music alone. I felt dead inside as if I wasn't really me.

But even in the darkest moments there was a thread of energy around me that seemed to say – you're a soul, keep on moving, keep on believing and in time, as time always does, the road will reveal things to you … the journey will become clearer in God's light. Remember who you are, remember what you've seen and witnessed as a child. There is another plan, a reconfiguration at play. One day in time you will see and understand. The journey is long and homeward bound. Your role here is played out and done. It's time to move on.

Though life was not the same, I couldn't believe that he was really going to leave us that way. This wasn't the man I knew who loved us and had always protected us. How would we survive this? His brother rang from New York one night – I couldn't speak as tears were just running down my face like a waterfall.

Mark couldn't stay with us – he had lessons to learn. In time, more than just his talent would be tested. I kept thinking about loyalty, grace, compassion, integrity, honour – the wave kept resounding. I felt numb emotionally and so cold. I kept dreaming of a cluttered house over and over again. I looked at happy couples as if I were viewing them on a movie screen – it was almost surreal. I wasn't bitter about love, I was just shell-shocked. The bullet had lodged itself deep inside, immoveable and invisible to the naked eye.

I was moving away, gravitating to a new level, a kind of foreign land that was unexplored. I was leaving behind friends, lessons, memories, music, art and creativity that will remain indelibly imprinted forever in my psyche. He was gone, quickly, impassionately, and everyone seemed to have their spin on this fairytale gone wrong.

'Oh, didn't you know he could be like that?'

'Oh, didn't you see it coming?'

I felt as if I had stepped outside of my physical form. Broken-hearted and off the rails. My daughter was my light, a jewel in the desert.

She hugged me and kissed me on the lips, and said, 'We will be alright, Mummy.' Her big blue eyes were like water that reflected my tear-soaked eyelashes.

I think about it now, years later, and realise that we are all tested, life has its lessons and it's how we deal with them that exposes our true colours, our soul.

My life had changed and the life of the singer/songwriter seemed to be eons away. The family had experienced me singing but the dream had faded. The opportunities felt flimsy in comparison to being there for the most important reason – watching and nurturing my daughter. I suffered depression for a while, smoked and drank to escape from being abandoned.

I had pawned the ring he gave me for $70, so I could pay the rent. I've sometimes wondered who purchased it, where it landed. I felt tortured but at the lowest point I felt a sense of the divine and that God would be there. I don't know how I had reasoned that but although we were living on a razor's edge, there was a feeling of warmth within. My one regret is that we had to leave the house that we moved into with Mark. I felt I had let the family down whose house I had rented. Things became out of control and I had to completely re-invent myself.

One day, the girl that had asked to speak to Mark on the phone was at my brother-in-law's studio – many, many, moons later. Upon walking in and hearing her spoken voice illuminating from another room, I could actually see an aura envelop me. It was white at first and then turned pink. I couldn't understand why I would be covered in the colour of love when I had felt so sabotaged by her and Mark. I didn't wish her ill and was aware that it takes two to tango but the colour of the aura around me years later blew me away. It felt like it was also a recognition of my soul's memory that appeared before me as I entered the house.

Love has no time; it's endless, and spans our cosmic universe and our hearts are like a key signature that opens a door to tell the story of a soul's lifetime.

The numbness continued. I could still hear music when I chose to but living that life didn't pay the bills. I did backing sessions in my friend's studio because it was an opportunity to keep a finger in the pie. My soul was ripped apart emotionally but the world couldn't see it. It was well disguised until I sang.

Doves cry

Not long after Mark and I separated, I went to a clairvoyant that I had found in the local newspaper to see if she could tell me anything of value. Little did I know she would become a great mentor of mine. I had seen her a couple of times before and felt that she was very talented as a psychic medium. She was connected to the Victorian Spiritualist Union with churches throughout Victoria.

I went to see her, bleary-eyed and forlorn. She saw that the relationship was in ruins and also told me that there were guides who wanted to work with me.

I had no idea what she meant. 'Work with me' – was that some kind of joke?

She said, 'Spirit people would work with you.'

I was taken aback! 'Um, okay, sure.'

At that point in time, I was so heartbroken I think anyone could have said anything and I would have said, 'Oh, okay then.'

I was in the land of broken-hearted blues. She took my phone number and she told me things that she could not possibly have known. I was living in the share household with my daughter, which was a challenge in itself, being the eldest there and the only one with a child. I sometimes wondered if I were living in a dream and that soon I would awaken and Mark would return and we would be the happy family we were before, with music playing and laughter and country drives and my soulmate there by my side, watching out for us.

No … think again … wrong … my life had taken a sudden sharp turn, irreversible and swift. I didn't want this life, I wanted my old life back with love in it. I wanted the security, the music and art, the conversations and I wanted my soulmate, my life force, to return and love me like he used to love me. I felt like the entire universe was sucking my soul into a mushed oblivion that was me. I lost myself somewhere there and found it in a little girl, my daughter. We would survive better, stronger. I didn't know how but we would. These guides, these spirit people, did they know how I was feeling? Were they somehow watching us?

They say one door opens and another one closes. Oh, so true. This was the end of me and the beginning of a new me. I had been depressed but not suffered with depression, although I had a bout of anorexia. Shaye, my daughter, was my light and through it all I would be a mother first. I would, and always will be, a mother first.

Jill, my mentor, had been a primary school teacher. Around the time of her retirement, she started hearing things. When she went to the supermarket, for instance, she heard, 'Oh, that man's having an affair,' and 'Oh, that child has pneumonia,' and 'She's just come back from overseas'.

At first, she thought she had gone mad. She eventually found herself at a Spiritualist Church, they told her she was clairaudient and out of control. The term 'clairaudient' refers to hearing Spirit. She learned to control this and became a wonderful teacher. Many students of hers will attest to her wonderful training and it was an honour to be part of her group. No money was involved – just those invited who she felt were attuned to Spirit. Her ways were traditional, healing and authentically from Spirit. She was in recession from bowel cancer – the medications that she had taken had wrecked her teeth, but her soul shone. She was as wise as wisdom could be kind and sweet, and was taken from this world all too soon. You might say she was the real McCoy.

She once told me in a reading that my grandfather (here he was again) was telling her that I would be going camping. Just out of the blue – camping.

I said, 'Oh no, not this city slicker, I don't think so, I wouldn't know the first thing about camping.'

I believed Jill to be very talented, but just couldn't see that I would ever, in my wildest dreams, go camping. Besides, I couldn't afford it. It was six months later that my dear friends invited myself and my daughter to camp at Apollo Bay. It's the only time I've ever been camping in my life. Ha ha, Jill was spot on. Yes, Grandpa saw it too. We were going camping, and it was a hoot.

I worked with Jill in a Psychic Mediumship Circle for around nine months. I liken it to the time a baby is in the womb. My life changed unequivocably. I was sensing Spirit, a joy had returned.

My daughter and I moved out of the share household and we got a second-storey flat in Hawthorn where we could see the treetops and roofs of houses stretching out for miles. Even the church steeple was visible. I worked in a government job. Life was back on track and I was developing my psychic abilities and enjoying it.

In those days, word got around that I was psychic and I even did a reading during a lunchbreak for a colleague in her car. I remember feeling more sensitive than usual to familiar things. A neighbour who lived downstairs came over for a coffee one day – he was sitting in a chair and I on the couch. We chatted about this and that … tra la la, and then he said he must be off to work or he'll be late, and off he went. I closed the door and, exhausted from working myself, I sat down on the chair he had been sitting in when all of a sudden I jumped out of the chair like hit by a flash of lightening. I had just sensed that he was interested in me, in that all too familiar way that guys get interested. Oh my God, was this also a forerunner of psychic ability? Oh my!

Dreams

Who looks outside, dreams; who looks inside, awakens.
Carl Jung

I was still juggling working, mothering, singing and wedding gigs. Again, I don't know how I squeezed it all in but there were the demands of modern living – rent, school fees and food. I had a wonderful family and they were very supportive. They didn't really talk much about the psychic world but given our background and events that my family could speak of, they didn't rule it out.

When I began work at a call centre, one of the team managers who knew I'd come from a musical background said, 'Welcome to the real world.'

That's exactly what it was like. There were up to 120 calls a day, maybe even more. By the time it had reached 5pm, I didn't want to speak any more.

The world was turning. The rent was high and we didn't have much left over to spend. My ability as a reader was still developing and a friend from the call centre would look after Shaye on a Saturday when I was in the psychic development class. Shaye was still at primary school wearing a secondhand uniform and I was learning to live in a world that was new to me with office etiquette, a database and the general public. Romance was on the backburner. Music would still be a passionate love of mine and I juggled work with singing at weddings and also a motown act – joy had returned. I had found my feet again and felt comfortable as a single mother. This drill lasted for around five years. I had finally built a new life.

I noticed that my dream life had begun to take on a new deeper level as I encountered some prolific dreams. Many people dream of their loved ones who have crossed over. When we are in a dream state, it's easier for them to communicate with us because our conscious mind is resting.

As we develop psychically, we never know who may pop into a dream. While in the little flat in Hawthorn, I had a big dream.

In the early hours of the night, I awoke bolt upright. It was a nightmare. A woman's car had gone under the water and she had yelled out, 'Oh God, someone help me.'

The water was so dark. She was a stocky woman in my dream and there was a 'golden light' around her car. I had seen the car submerge into the water and felt her terror.

Upon awaking, I took a look around, the room was silent, it was a dream. My heart was racing as it seemed so real. But I said to myself, it's just a dream and I went back to sleep.

The next morning, I told my daughter about the dream that I'd had, how I saw a car drive into the water and that a woman was trapped inside and cried out for help. I think the lucidity of it scared me, how real it was. I felt as if it were me in a strange way so that I could feel exactly what she felt. Tuned in.

I was rehearsing that day, songs were in my head and I had to be on the other side of town. I grabbed my bag and keys, got in the car, and turned on the radio. The news was on – a woman's car went under the water at Werribee Dam.

'What?'

I sat dumbfounded in the car for about 10 minutes, thinking about my dream before driving away. It was as if a signal had been sent out that night and anyone whose antenna was on was going to receive it.

I followed this story – an ambulance driver saved her life. Apparently he was with a group of friends and they were talking about what they would do if someone's car went under water. Can you believe it?

I looked at it like this – he was being prepared by the universe, they were sending their angels through. Two cars witnessed her going into the dam and they stopped. The ambulance driver just happened to be driving by at the time and they flagged him over. What an angel, and a team of guardian angels. It wasn't her time. Months later, I remembered the golden light I vividly saw in the dream.

This was another insight. Dreams and dreaming, psychic dreams, they had other colours and a language all of their own. Lucid in nature as if I were there because they were so visual.

What I have learned, I have shared. I believe that's important so we can leave this world a better place. A sister had a dream one night that there were white tiles behind the oven in the house in East Malvern. She was given this piece of information from my Grandmother Ruby, who was deceased, discarnate. Inspired by this information, a board was removed from the back and sides of the oven and ... voila ... there they were, the white tiles. The proof is in the pudding. Well, in this case it was in the white tiles.

We were all stunned as that piece of information was so left of centre with white tiles. But my sister was delighted she had been validated, as were we all, and we learned to trust. Trust what is given.

Trusting information is key: trusting our intuition and that what we are feeling has a reason. It could be simple things like not trusting a particular person and knowing that they would not keep confidential information to themselves. Trusting our gut, and that sometimes things take time to unwind and reveal themselves. Some also advocate that knowing ourselves is important and being truthful to ourselves in our own heart of hearts assists us in knowing another.

In my early twenties, I had a recurring dream that I was invited to travel up a staircase. I was always frightened by this and would never completely walk the entire way. There was a woman at the end of the staircase inviting me to travel further. I would usually awaken from this dream and think that it was unusual that I was dreaming it again with the same visual over and over, never reaching the end of the staircase. I realise now it was probably part of an initiation to conquer the fear of the unknown. To trust and go with the flow. I believe it was Spirit working in a dream, wanting to work with me and giving me a sense of the hereafter. Once I became more connected to the realm of spirit, this dream vanished.

My dream world continued to open up and reveal stories of other souls and their journeys as well.

Moving on

Life was about to take another turn for myself and my daughter. The bills were mounting and it was hard to survive. The owner of the apartment wished to move back into it so I applied to co-op community housing and we got in. With trepidation, we moved. But it was a relief as previously there was little left over after each pay to live on. At least we would have a chance to grow with a little extra money.

It was another milestone but we were ready. The new house was brilliant – it was spacious and we even had a garden. I could afford to study and work at the hospital nearby. My daughter was in the middle of high school. When we first moved in, I kept seeing a vision of a guy lying in the garage. This continued for about two weeks. Then one morning, as I was about to go to work, there was a young man lying on the ground of the garage. I thought he was dead. Fear gripped me and I slowly walked towards him as if I were walking in slow motion. He then awoke – he was an addict who had parked himself in my garage. Thankfully, he didn't return but my daughter's bicycle mysteriously disappeared a week later. It was a great house but the location was a bit dubious. We struggled so much financially that I once had to go to the library to go to the toilet. The drive to the call centre was gruelling and I was becoming so drained on the phones. I prayed and prayed and believed that things would improve. I had a strong and enduring team of friends who supported me and had faith in my soul.

I dated a few guys but nothing ever eventuated. Once they knew I was a medium, they thought I was a crackpot. Even if I predicted something that came true, they put it down to coincidence. I remember telling one of the guys I dated that he had tiles outside his house.

He said, 'Oh, you must have driven by.'

I was reading at the time for friends for nothing, just to gain some experience. Eventually, I did readings at some of the New Age stores. But the guys I dated still thought it was too far a stretch to really believe that it was possible for people to be in contact with those who had passed.

Until I was doing platform demonstrations at the spiritualist churches in Victoria, this disbelief would upset me. My sister Leigh 'got it'. She was the only one in the early days who understood the frustrations and letdowns. I think it was because she had suffered the same misrepresentation, was sensitive to energy and was also a single mother who understood the financial and emotional turbulence.

I dreamed a dream

Oh my God ... I heard a gunshot ... just keep running ... there seemed to be white bandages around them ... I was flying above this person ... there was a long stretch of road. Oh my God, I could feel what they were feeling. They felt so guilty someone had been shot and it wasn't them and it wasn't their fault. Just run, keep running ...

I felt as if a portal had been ripped open and I could see a vision of someone who was running for their life. I also felt as if there were a sense of angels on their side, as if my vision was not mine alone but that there was an intelligence in the universe that was aware of what was happening.

This was a high-profile case. It was weeks later that I heard about it on the news. This woman was indeed running for her life in the desert on a long stretch of road after her partner had been shot.

I felt as if I were part of the eyes of a team that was urging this woman to keep going. She did but her partner had vanished. She was running but her heart was breaking. She was trying to save her own life, knowing she and her partner had met with foul play. I could sense it as if I were her but as if I were also adding fuel to the run – keep moving, keep going. As if there were a heart in the universe that was somehow acknowledging the sense of it all as the run continued. She was going to survive. There was a force within her; around her.

It was as I had dreamed – she did escape and did run for her life. There were also white bandages around her as she had escaped after being tied up. The case with her boyfriend's body continued, and his body still hasn't been found. I could feel her terror and bravery as I flew above her in the dream to keep her surging forward, for the love of the universe was on her side. My heart and soul goes out to her to this very day – I think of her and the forces above and beyond. For surely her partner would have wanted her to survive, to run, as she ran through the rage of losing him, his death informing her, encouraging each pace faster and faster, moving her closer to freedom.

It was one soul dreaming of another needing help, yet the dream was coming through me like a witness of the divine weaving its web of wonder. I felt connected … and was aware that we are more than the physical reality, more than the surface; there were deeper layers that we as humans could transit to.

We can fly and perhaps millions of people all over the world dreamt of her that night, perhaps millions of people heard the cry and felt the sting of injustice through a dream. And we all still do dream those dreams because we are connected, and like the eye of an eagle that can see in the distance for nearly eight miles, we too can do that but it's with our eyes closed.

Faith

This is based on a true story but modified to protect the participants. In August 2009, I was at home one night when I clairaudiently became aware of a question from Spirit.

We are giving you a dream soon. Will you do something about it?

I replied yes.

Days later, again I heard the question.

We will be giving you a dream soon. Will you do something about it?

I replied in my mind, answering the question again. Yes, okay, yes I will.

Then a day or so later, again I heard the question. This time, it felt really serious.

We are giving you a dream soon. Will you do something about it?

My demeanour had changed. I knew it was serious, more so than I could imagine. This time, my heart seemed to be more actively involved in the exchange.

Yes, I will do something, yes, I will. I will, it's important and I will.

A week later, I dreamt that someone had been murdered in a vicious way and thrown down a well. The unusual part was that I received a name in the dream as well. I dreamt that my sister had been murdered and I awoke in shock. I didn't understand it initially but the scene gave me my sister's name because in the dream she had been murdered and her name was the same as the surname of the family that had been slain. I knew what the spirit world was trying to impress on me – there was a family involved, sharing the same name as my sister. They were showing me a family connection. I felt shock and horror as if it had happened in my own family.

At the end of the dream, I saw a man standing behind a curtain with a young girl. I knew in my dream that the man who had committed the crime was an uncle in the family. In my dream, an aunty knew more about him, but she had died too.

I had seen a carpet with a blood stain on it. The carpet was geometrical in my dream. Whether the carpet in the house was geometrical as a matter of fact, I will never know but the information that Spirit was giving was about the carpet. I had seen him in a house with blinds and a girl was standing next to him, a young girl. As the blinds closed, I awoke. The dread I sensed was so intense and my heart was pounding.

I must have woken from my dream around 5am but I couldn't get back to sleep as it seemed so real. I recognised the dream as psychic as it was so lucid and real. I was really shaken. I couldn't really make sense of it other than knowing it was really serious and significant. I stayed awake, frightened, for some time but eventually fell back to sleep.

In the morning, the first thing that came to mind was the dream as it played over in my mind. It was important to remember details, I kept thinking to myself, so I made some notes.

It suddenly dawned on me. I felt sick as I remembered the question weeks before. And I also knew the murder the spirit world was impressing on me. I recognised the case.

I was in a daze for a day. I envisaged a grandmother so sad, with her head hanging so lowly. I wondered what the vision of the girl with the uncle in the end of the dream meant as I saw the vision over and over. My heart was breaking. I didn't really want to investigate the media reports as I wanted to be as unbiased as I could about what Spirit had given me. I had made a vow to them that I would do something.

I knew the murder case that the spirit world was trying to impress upon me. I was so touched they visited me. And the stain on the carpet. Who knows if the geometrical design was crucial or if they were impressing on me that the stain was on the floor? The vision was so strong. It was of utmost importance to give the information to the authorities and they could do what they had to do with it. As it turned out, the stain was imperative to the case. It showed evidence.

Cautious with my dream, I spoke to my mother and a friend of hers whose son-in-law was a detective. He told me how to go about it – to report it with a made-up name. I was so nervous that the first time I rang the number my hands were shaking so much the call dropped out.

I wasn't sure if what I had dreamt was right or not, but because of the sequence of the events, the information and the intensity of it, coupled with the question of 'doing something with the information' before I even had the dream, I went with my heart.

I tried again. This time, early evening, I was put through to an officer and gave them the information I had. I felt foolish at first but as I recalled the vision I knew it was from Spirit so, whether it made sense or not, I gave it.

It took years for the case to unfold but it turned out the police did find a blood stain that assisted the case. They found it on the garage floor. Whether my dream helped or not I don't know – perhaps I will never know. It was interesting that I saw a stain in my dream and now in hindsight I'm glad I provided the information, although it seemed small at the time and almost insignificant. Others, too, as it turned out suspected the uncle.

This was one of the worst murders the country has ever known. A family slain and a daughter surviving, whom the uncle took in to live with him.

It must have been about a week after I gave the information that I was at home when I felt the strangest sensation. It was the presence of many in the room with a feeling of such gratitude and love. I could sense the family, the souls, like shadows of those who had passed. I felt truly humbled. I had kept my promise. They knew I would. Time stood still, no need for words or thoughts – just the presence of spirit to spirit and all was known, all the thoughts captured in the essence of moments, sacrifice, love, understanding, heart to heart.

The love for their daughter and concern for her as she was taken in by the uncle was strong enough to break through the veil of death. The untimely departure and savage slayings of their bodies couldn't stop their souls from trying to protect her. Love was turning the tide, it was electric and yet so soft and deep. If I could see the daughter, I would tell her that she is loved more than she realises. She is treasured and cherished and the love they have for her is still alive. More than a human soul can interpret. Though every day she must be sad for the loss of her family, every day they are here in her heart. I imagine in heaven that the family rejoice as they are so happy there is a victory for them through the miracle of love.

Interpreter

2012 November. A beautiful young woman appeared in my dream. She was dead and she couldn't believe she had been stabbed. She was communicating to me that there was another friend of hers in the dream and she felt so guilty she had left her friend when they had been out.

The two girls had been out together and one had gone her way, leaving the other. The discarnate spirit couldn't believe she had crossed over in such a violent way. It wasn't her time. There would be talk of a car for a while. I could see in my dream it had been abandoned.

Then I awoke. I was at the time living with a good friend, another medium – we were in the same circle and had remained friends. Like attracts like. No news had broken yet. In the morning I spoke of the dream. Later on, I realised through the media that a girl had gone missing, then a car was found abandoned. The search was on and it became a high-profile case. I knew it was the girl in my dream.

This time, there was no damning evidence, nothing to pass on but she had visited or I had travelled to where I was needed. I sent her all the love I could and to this day I remember, and send love out to her family and friends. It wasn't her time. I remember we communicated telepathically through the dream, I could see her looking radiant the night she appeared in my dream. It was like she had woken up on the other side, still confused but beautiful. I hope I had a light around me and that in that other space and time there was knowledge that she and her loved ones will meet again, without pain or sorrow, without regret or anguish. Pure love and the complete happiness and joy of the reuniting of spirits of mother and daughter, father and daughter, friends, cousins. What was broken then unbroken and mended through time. Forever and ever and ever.

Belief

This story has been modified to protect the recipients.

I worked with Rochelle as a singer and it was a privilege. She and her husband had worked the club scene for years and made a living out of music. I recall not long after we met we struck up a keen friendship and she confided in me. She told me they lived in an area where there was a keen birdlife and had two children.

One morning her husband and two of the children were in their car when it was tragically hit by another. Her husband and one of her daughters were killed in the accident. The Funeral was a haze for her unable to speak because of the intensity of the loss and grief as friends and family flocked to her side.

She returned home to an empty house after a small gathering. It was unbearable without them.

On the afternoon of the funeral she'd been home for about half an hour or so and as she walked into the kitchen area she saw two white birds circling around the room making five or so circles then fly outside. In all the time she had lived there it had never happened before. It stopped her in her tracks as love pierced her heart.

She felt her spirit and a sense that somewhere sometime in the future they would be together again and that at that moment in time their souls were locked together through love. She took this as a divine sign that love never dies and as the birds flew out she remembered feeling filled with the essence that this spiritual sign was enough to ease her broken spirit for the meantime and fill her with the notion that they were living on; waiting for her when her time would come. They would meet again.

Perhaps from a philosophical point of view, we are reminded that we belong to the spirit world as we do to the earthly – we enter a knowing that belongs to us as spirits in both domains.

Talking with our loved ones who have crossed over has been around since time immemorial. People have reported speaking with spirits, dreaming of visions that came true and warnings of comings to be by angels. In the Bible there are stories of angels guiding men and women. The mystical is part of our story here on earth and as the saying goes, 'We are spirits having a physical experience'.

But more than that love is speaking in a language that bears no physical words but perhaps in its purer sense this is God's work; the Creator's work. A knowing in the heart from one who has loved another and that nature speaks for us when we are without words in a deeper tone.

I sat so still as Rochelle recounted the story; she was gifting me with the knowledge that the divine had played its part. Many times through the journey the many reads that I had done for people who came to me had their own precious gems and inner knowledge that life and love continue on past earthly death. They carried these treasures with them as some would speak of it and others wouldn't in their day to day existence as they feared rebuttal if they gave over their evidence of soul survival.

They never had to convince me, time after time I was touched and almost reborn at the same instance with the presence that the soul intertwining miraculously brought to them. Comfort and peace. They were teaching me. I was humbled in their presence to be led into their world and hear their stories was the greatest gift and honour.

I understood the skeptic's point of view, I got it. They couldn't see the spirit world, they wanted proof. They hadn't experienced a Near Death Experience, they had no visions of an afterlife or any type of strong psychic sense they could pin a conclusion to. So therefore it didn't exist. At first it was a difficult atmosphere to be around but I found myself usually making little to no comment at all. I also found it hard when confronted with very angular and sharp beliefs that religion was such and such, and as for mediums and psychics they were just make believe.

Mystical

Reading for another person was a privilege and I made a pledge with myself that if there ever came a time that information wasn't coming through then I would leave it behind knowing that I had served my time for spirit as best I could. I recognised the need for a deeper understanding and had a curiosity for religion and philosophy wanting to marry these to my meaning of the spiritual. I studied Spiritualism and researched the pioneers interested in the history, beliefs and the principles but I also had a keen interest in the major religions of the world. Love was the mirror that was gifting me access to the interior world of the soul. The interior world of the soul was where the creator could speak to all of us.

I studied Christianity also and discovered its richness. From studying I learned that the disciples understood Christ as a mighty prophet, healer, teacher but they didn't fully comprehend that he was destined to be put to death and rise again. The meaning gleaned, that there is life beyond death as powerful today for believers as it must have been for those experiencing the story for the first time. "Look at my hands and my feet. It is I myself! Touch me and see; a ghost does not have flesh and bones, as you see I have. " (Lk 24:29).

Luke's Gospel shows us what it means to be faithful to God in a world addicted to wealth and power. Faith is the birds flying into the room, faith is the tide reaching the shore, faith is a baby being born in the midst of war. Faith is that love isn't temporary in the universe of mankind. Faith is where the night sky reveals stars that speak of wonder and give hope of eternity.

The white birds that flew into the room had no idea what religion Rochelle believed in yet they somehow connected in emotionally reminding her that their souls lived on. As if the Creator were saying, I know you're hurting, I see through your eyes and I feel what you're feeling, love doesn't die.

Where there is faith there is an awareness of holiness
Paul Tillich

If I go to the temple

In their book *Encountering Religion* (2000), Ian. S. Markham and Tinu Ruparell inspired my work in philosophy and religious studies and helped me to understand as paraphrased here that religion can have a powerful impact on a community and has been seen to educate the masses and to provide moral and ethical codes of conduct. Religion can also maintain cultural values and social linkages.

> *The purpose of all major religions is not to construct big temples on the outside, but to create temples of goodness and compassion inside, in our hearts.*
> **Dalai Lama**

In my faith visit to a Hindu temple while studying religion, I was moved by the kindness and compassion of others. The following extract is from my journal.

> As I left the encounter I was filled with a sense of compassion for the other. I felt an interconnectedness. I felt that a spiritual dimension was opened up for me by the visit and this had enriched me. I felt a sense of the mystical and history mixed together in the stories I was told. I was impressed by Ravi's devotion and the devotion of the Hindu priest. I was shown kindness and that touched me in a simple and yet profound way. I could see a treasure in the worship, I could see that it brought comfort and pleasure for the devotees. To have inner

peace was comforting for me as I knelt praying in a temple that I didn't belong to and yet I still felt as if God were present and listening to my prayer. I could see that religion gives meaning to life, it's a source of life. I felt images of their deities swirling around in my head on clouds and visions of music interweaving to create beautiful melodies that were special and reverent. I saw that a religious experience could play an important role in my subconscious to inform my conscious. Symbols were playing in my mind, creating archetypes that I could recall later, perhaps much later in my life where I might be in need of divine assistance.

I felt privileged to be able to walk into the temple and although I couldn't speak to the priest in his own language, it was amazing to be given a tour of the sacred space in such a manner. My personal inner experience of this encounter was divine. I was immersed in the legends and myths. Finding God here in the temple was finding God within myself in the sacred space of the other while with reverence they were unlocking their most 'holy of holies'.

I recognised a common humanity and search for a higher dimension of the sacred. I recognised a sense of committing to my fellow man and embracing a flexible approach to understand the divine in all religions.

A flexible approach is called for to understand the divine in all religions. I need to consider the other's viewpoint as seriously as I consider my own. That understanding of spiritual presence is where spiritual care takes its stance. I need to engage; with contemplation I can be 'in awe'. Beliefs, culture and rituals can be divisive and could spark superiority without recognition of a common humanitarian thread. Commitment to understanding and embracing differences can be cathartic and empowering. In all faiths many changes have occurred throughout the time of its presence in the world. Understanding difference is important in any provision of interfaith spiritual care. These differences can give us a rich and interesting diversity to call upon. These differences should be nurtured and honoured as part of the other's fundamental human right and core belief system. Spiritual care crosses religious faiths and boundaries, recognised in the sacred presence of the other to whom I'm relating. Sensitivity and humility can foster presence to open a channel to enquire. I can be aware of my personal beliefs but not let them get in the way; for I should be self-aware enough to have the respect the other deserves. Humility cannot be technically taught but it will assist me in appreciating the other, and their ways of thinking. I need to be on guard to continually reflect and critique. For I could hold that space for another, I could be that conduit where they can open their heart and speak and, before I know it, I may offer some comfort and a sense of the divine within.

It seems unavoidable then that as we merge closer globally, we affect each other. It's no surprise that we bring our culture, beliefs, mythologies, religions and knowledge – we can inspire and inform each other as humans, that divine spark within as spiritual beings in a physical form.

And if I go to the Temple
to eat the food and drink the wine.
and if I fall at the temple
in search of something so divine
will it lead me back to you
all the colors that you possess
will it lead me back
Lyrics Ronda Robertson

Frequency

The Merriam Webster dictionary defines clairaudient as 'the power or faculty of hearing something not present to the ear but regarded as having objective reality'. This is from the French word *clair*, which means 'clear' and the word *audience* meaning 'hearing'.

Once while doing a platform demonstration, standing in front of a group of people communicating with the spirit world, I saw a blue aura next to a lady in the back row of about 30 people. I asked her to stand up as I had a message for her. She was happy to stand even though that can be confronting in itself. I clairaudiently heard Spirit say to me, 'Theodora is an important name in the family.'

Now I have learnt to trust these messages. So I faithfully said to this lady, 'I'm being told that Theodora is an important name in the family.'

She said, 'My grandmother's name is Theodora and my grandfather's name is Theodore.'

Mmm, thank you, Spirit … what a beautiful message to transfer across for this lady. I felt so humbled.

I'm simply doing the job, that's all, and transferring the messages across. It's emotional. I had worked as a professional singer – perhaps that helped. I had learnt how to separate instruments and how to construct music. I could hear it in my mind and was able to sing harmonies. I could hear music on the radio and I could hear it from within. I was able to separate sound. That sound that was from outside of me and the melodies from inside my mind.

Music has a frequency, and differing sounds translate different moods – hypnotic, calm, ambient to loud, aggressive, warlike, tribal.

It might be blues, jazz, funk, soul or even the intertwining of Celtic rhythms intricately woven that entice us to move, dance, love or inspire. I'm aware of my voice because I'm a singer. I'm aware of what my voice can do before I speak, from the point of view of using the voice as an instrument. One night while singing a Kasey Chambers song, I thought I needed to sound more hypnotic while singing this. Only moments later while singing, I nearly nodded off and quickly had to snap back to reality. Just imagine the singer on stage slipping off to sleep – not a good look! This experience, however, had a profound effect on me – the power of sound.

So when later I began reading for people, I was aware of another sound. The voice of spirit people, discarnate souls. To hear without the same frequency music has, but to hear messages nonetheless. To hear, to interpret the message and to translate that message to the living.

It's amazing. I've had people tell me that's my gut instinct. Well ... actually no, I'm hearing spirit talk, I'm tuning into that 'frequency'. Yes, you need to trust your soul with what you're hearing. The veil between one world is lifted and communication is possible. It's a new language, where the heart and mind work with souls this side and souls in the world of spirit on the other side.

Dad

Dad died in 2009 of lung cancer. He rapidly declined, he had lost a lot of weight prior to his diagnosis and had smoked since he was 16 years of age.

Dad had been diagnosed with a hilar mass in the lung, an abnormality in one or both of the hilar lymph nodes in the lungs. It usually indicates cancer.

Mum kept saying, 'I think he will go quickly.' In fact, she was right as the time from when he was diagnosed until he passed was only months.

I always had an alarm clock near my bed as I was worried I would sleep in and miss an early nursing shift. One night after Dad was diagnosed, I had set the alarm clock for the early morning as the early shift begins at 0700 hours, as many thousands upon thousands of nurses will know.

I awoke as I normally did but for some reason the alarm clock was much further away. I got up in a kind of daze in the morning like I usually do and went to the bathroom. I noticed the alarm clock there and turned off the alarm, but 'hang on', I never put the clock there.

I was stunned. I knew that it was a message for Dad, he was in fact leaving soon. To this day I know I never put the clock in the bathroom near the sink. I cannot explain this – I don't sleep walk, I never have. The clock moved to another room in the house 8 weeks before he died. If I was entranced to move it, I have absolutely no recognition of it at all. I kissed the clock, tears streaming, knowing what was to come and moved it back to my room.

I asked my daughter when I got home, 'Did you move the alarm clock?'

She replied, 'What are you talking about?'

I asked again, 'Did you move the alarm clock in my room?'

She replied, 'No, why? What are you talking about?'

I said, 'The alarm clock was in the bathroom when I got up this morning. I never put it there. I think it's about Grandpa; he will be leaving this world sooner than we think.'

I knew it, I could feel it. He would be leaving, his soul would return to the Great Spirit.

'I never moved it,' my daughter said.

My daughter and I started crying. It felt like we were in some kind of movie and I knew no one would believe me. I felt crazy. I told one friend, tears pouring down my face. It was a message he was leaving soon, that he didn't have long; Mum was right.

He'd had open heart surgery with four bypasses in his fifties but by 77 years, his time had come. He was ready. As his body withered away and he was lying in bed before being moved into palliative care, my sister asked him what he wanted us to do with his ashes. I couldn't believe she had asked him that question but both of them were so similar, with an enigmatic Taurus personality, so down-to-earth and so funny.

From his death bed, Dad answered, 'Listen, love, just go with the Tobin Brothers Funeral Package, $1999.'

Yep, classic, that's what he said. We both just laughed, tears were streaming down my face.

He wasn't scared. He said, 'I've seen them, they have come to visit.'

He meant his relatives from the other side. There was a presence in the room but, during this time, I was so overcome with the fact that he was dying that it was difficult to process anything else. This was days before he was moved into palliative care. He had been a funeral director, after all. He knew how to organise and plan for the event. The only thing that was different was that it was his turn this time. My sister took it pretty well and being the realist, she organised the whole thing.

As he spoke about his visitors, I could feel his sister Bonnie's presence in the room. I had that familiar feeling that I experienced as a child in the funeral parlour, the thinning of the veil … There was that sensation of the link between this world and the next, just like it had been when I was a little girl in the funeral parlour and witnessed the body in the coffin.

Mystical

We were getting ready to lose a major force in our lives. Good and bad, he had his moments – embarrassment, chip-on-the-shoulder, disestablishment, political right wing, small business rants. He was now moving towards the divine, the other side. He had no fear; faith kept him strong.

When I first started reading, Dad's curiosity was spiked. My family were aware that I was in a development circle and since we had a history of spiritual occurrences happening, I wasn't overly surprised when Dad asked me to do a reading for him.

He said, 'I hope you do it with a Bible.'

We sat in one of the rooms with the piano adjacent to us. Dad had an ashtray nearby and assumed a comfortable position in a chair. I sat on a sofa and closed my eyes to see what would be transferred from the spirit world.

I told him I could see a house in the country. It was my first vision and they were showing me what appeared to be a field of wheat blowing in the air. I could hear a voice saying to me they were surprised that he didn't have more flowers growing in the garden.

I looked over to see him, and he was listening quietly so I resumed the read.

Then, slowly, I saw black shiny shoes hazily coming through a vision and was told of a spearmint-tasting sweet that someone used to like.

As I glanced over for confirmation, I saw that Dad was becoming emotional. Yes, he believed it was his father coming through.

He said, 'Yes, Dad used to have shiny shoes. I remember as a child, him polishing them and he would have spearmint sweets.'

'He is now saying the word "dolly" to me.' I looked over at my father and asked him, 'Did you have a dolly?'

I noticed tears streaming down his face. 'Dolly was the name of a horse my father had.'

His father had come through to him. It was unexpected and it was early in my development – and it can be difficult to read for family or friends as we can't be as objective. Yet his father had come through, and Dad was grateful and moved. I felt I had done a service. He lost his father to leukaemia when he was six years old. Although Dad was charismatic and intelligent, he went off the rails as a teenager and ran away from home and was raised by an uncle. He never had the opportunity to glean the wisdom from a father who had left too early.

The spirit world went on to say that he must visit his sister Bonnie and that it was urgent that he do so. She had a leg amputated due to diabetes before she passed three months later.

For a large part of the time Dad and I clashed, as he was down to earth and practical and I was airy and artistic, but here we shared a great commune with Spirit. I believe he gained insight and depth into the power of love from the other side.

We moved Dad into palliative care and visited continually as families do before he passed.

Julie, my sister and I were talking together in the dining room. It was the week before he died.

Julie said, 'It feels different, it feels like he's on a different level, Roni.'

A few minutes later, I looked up and saw a flash of my grandfather and a light in the doorway that was right in front of me. Doorways are powerful – there is much energy as people move to and fro through them. When I saw my grandfather standing there, I also saw an image of hundreds of birds, flying out as well. I could sense the meaning.

His time was coming. It was a truly mystical and moving moment. I was beyond tears as I stood next to my sister.

Julie was right ... he was moving to another level and was not long for this world. His transition was about to occur. I was moved by what I had seen and, in a kind of trance-like state, I said, 'Yeah.'

He wasn't long for this world. There was a comfort about the space, a softness, a lingering of energy. There was a feeling of souls he once knew, collecting on the other side, getting ready to take him across. It wouldn't be long.

My mother still misses him terribly – it's hard for those left behind. He was so funny. My sister said she saw him in the lounge room the day after he passed, standing in his old check shirt and pants still smoking. I wondered why I didn't at that point see him or hear from him? I was pretty disappointed as wasn't that supposed to happen to me as a medium?

In hindsight now, I would say to you, Spirit will communicate in their own way, don't force it, it will happen when it's supposed to. It's sacred.

Around the time that Dad passed, I had been dating a guy and when Dad passed I texted him to let him know. He was clearly shaken with the news and hoped I was okay.

I was staying at Mum's place as we now had the job of caring for her. She was independent but, of course, when one parent dies, it's only natural to care for the other and we knew it was what Dad wanted. He wanted to be more than sure she would be cared for. It was six weeks after his death when I was awoken from my sleep in the front room of the house. I felt someone poke me lightly on the shoulder, saying 'seeing someone'.

The poke in the shoulder had definitely woken me up, but I wondered how I could be poked in the shoulder when I was alone. I was lying on my stomach and, as I suddenly woke up properly, I knew it was Dad. I wasn't scared and then I heard his voice, as clear and distinctive as if he were in the room, saying it to me … 'Seeing someone'.

As far as Dad was concerned, that was important enough a message for him to relay to me. It was my 'wake-up call'.

Two weeks later, I got the text after messaging the guy I was seeing. Not even a call. 'I'm seeing someone else' was what the guy I had been dating texted.

I laughed to myself through tears. *Yeah*, I thought, *my father already told me.*

He woke me up and told me that in the middle of the night six weeks after he died.

Love was breaking through the two worlds, telling me about something which I would learn in the coming weeks; however, it was more powerful than that. It was the connection, the miracle that death is not the final frontier, that we are loved beyond this realm, that those who go before us do know, do hear, do feel and love us as souls and will touch our hearts and minds and bring forth messages and ideas and revelations to help and heal. Something so powerful can't be bought, purchased materially – it's an interconnectedness that reminds us that the language of Spirit is where the heart lies.

It was beyond powerful, beyond words and the realm in which we reside. The power of love bonding us, moving us, driving home the reverence that we all share. The miracle of who we really are, what we really are. I was truly humbled by the presence and the power of the light of love.

Keep an open mind

Clairaudience plays a fundamental role in mediumship. While I was a student studying ceramics, I was standing waiting to cross a really busy road. Suddenly I could hear music playing from the outside into my left ear, almost like a transistor radio, like an orchestra playing. It was not like hearing a melody that you remember in your mind. This was like someone had just put a headphone onto my left ear and music was playing. Then it just as suddenly stopped. I will usually hear clairaudiently into my left ear. The day I heard the music was like Spirit fine-tuning my clairaudience.

I would like at this point to introduce another story about hearing clairaudiently. I earlier gave you an example of platform work and hearing Spirit give a name to me to pass on, so I'd like to include this.

It was another dream and I was flying near a concert stage. I felt as if I were in another country; the music was dynamic, there were three stages all at differing heights and a horn section on one stage, backing singers and soloists – the music was wonderful. Then my soul seemed to journey outside with a group of people – I was flying above them. It was interval and I could hear them talking about the songs.

'Oh, we better go back inside,' I heard one of them say.

I flew back inside and then I woke up. I was back in my conscious state. I laughed to myself, as I thought I had astral-travelled to see a concert somewhere, though I wasn't sure where. This was really cool and cheaper than having to pay for tickets.

My daughter had been out the night I had had that dream, and when she got home she asked me what I had done.

I said, 'Oh, I went to see a band.'

She said, 'You never said you were going out to see a band. Which one? Where?'

'Well, honey, it's kind of hard to explain but I think I astral-travelled and heard music last night.'

I believe it was Spirit opening up my clairaudient abilities. It was another wonderful experience.

At around the same time, early one Sunday morning, I was lying in bed and I heard the sound of what seemed to me to be angels singing. It was celestial in sound and feel. Now I know that sounds very far-fetched, and the sound was likened to the sound of a choir in a church. I knew at the time, however, that I was hearing something completely different and emanating from a differing source to that of normal sounds. It was incredibly beautiful and just as quickly as it had been heard it vanished, probably lasting for around half a minute but something I will never forget. Half a minute is a long time, really, to hear such an incredibly beautiful sound. It was angelic. I honestly felt I had been given a vision of the sound of angels. Exquisite.

Vision

When you see something that is not fixed to the earth, you will remember it and it will change the way you feel about Spirit, this dimension and other dimensions. It can occur when you are not expecting it and it will expand your view. I'm not the only one – the world is changing, views are changing, and we are evolving and growing into a newfound consciousness, one that we have always had. We are just learning to remember again.

In 2002 I started work at a major hospital in Melbourne. I started out in a clerical role before turning to nursing, a move I have always cherished. When I first interviewed, I really had never had any experience working in a role like the one I was going for in a busy metropolitan hospital. I dressed well, took a positive view of things and decided to get there early.

I sat waiting for my turn to be called in and walked down the corridor of the ward lined with hospital beds, and then I saw him. He was standing at the edge of the bed dressed in a brown suit and a hat. There was a light, yellow golden, and a veil between him and me. I was walking past a high dependency unit and could see through the windows into the room, which is not unusual as these patients need extra attention. I distinctly recall slowing down in speed and taking it all in. Initially, it was the hat that threw me. Then that familiar heart pounding came rushing in. Oh God, it's a spirit at the end of the bed, as clear as day. Of course, no one else could see it, they were all going about their business. I continued to walk into the room of the interview and it went well – I got the job. As I walked out of the room he had gone, and I had to just keep walking.

It wasn't the first time I would see things, auras or flashes of light in the hospital setting, but I chose to turn this particular skillset off while I was at work. Not because I didn't want to see but because I wanted to be professional and like everybody else there. I needed to focus on clinical skills, not spiritual matters at the time. It was like I was opening up to a different kind of energy, enabling me to view things from another perspective that included a spiritual faculty of awareness turned on.

Years later when I was nursing early one morning, however, I was assigned to a young girl. Her mother had been up all night crying as the young girl had been diagnosed with lung cancer. Any mother will know of the heartache one feels when a child is not well. She was a beautiful young girl and the nurse in charge of the shift thought I would be good looking after her on that particular day. Nursing shifts start early so by 0730 hours we would be ready to begin taking vital observations. The sun was slowly rising on that morning and as I walked into the room and saw her sitting up in bed I could see a red patch over her upper chest and as I stood behind her it was all orange. I could tell from the red patch that this was probably where the cancer was located. When I saw the orange colour, it felt like the colour was strong in her aura and there was a healing taking place. Her mother was beside herself and so weary from a night without much sleep and with much crying.

I introduced myself to her mother and said, 'Looks like you've had a rough night.'

'Yes, it's been like that.'

I asked the doctor covering the unit that morning where the growth was and it was where I had envisioned the red patch. I could only hope that I was right with the healing. Quite a lot of the doctors, surgeons and nurses I worked with believe in the afterlife. In my opinion, many of the people I worked with were true angels on earth and true healers.

As I've mentioned, before starting at the hospital, I worked in a call centre and on this particular occasion I was called into the room where my supervisor would give me an appraisal. The room was not well lit. I sat down and he began talking about my performance and stats. As he was speaking, I could see a yellow light around his head over his ears. When he was finished, I went back to my seat. The girl I sat next to knew of my extrasensory abilities, so I caught her attention and told her what I saw.

Mystical

She said, 'No way,' in this beautiful Anglo-Greek accent.

I said, 'Yes, that's what I saw, a yellow light around his head near his ears.'

We thought nothing of it. The next day my supervisor was off with an ear infection ... mmm.

My friend from the call centre and I were both shocked but we knew that was what I was seeing. These colours just appeared as I was sitting there. I have over time learnt to shut down as much as I have learnt to tune into this ability.

Pink

Reading auras is a gentle thing, and I'm glad that I've had the opportunity to develop it. It wasn't an instant development; it happened over time. I'm still learning and hope to never stop learning. There is another story of colour and aura reading but before I delve into this one, I just wanted to let you know that in order to see auras you don't need to be artistic. The colour is more of an energy; an energy of light. You do need to have patience and have faith in the spirit world because *when the heart's in the right place we see everything.*

After the split with Mark, he quickly got into another relationship and I really wished him well. I began another job and my daughter and I rented a small flat. I was moving on in my life and had begun doing small readings for friends, family and anyone else interested. I was loving this newfound faculty and was keen to develop it. I kept away from any venues that I thought Mark would be performing at for obvious reasons – I would only be upset if I saw him again.

It was about a year later that I finally decided to go to a gig and leave a card. It was kind of my way of saying goodbye and moving forward and also to let him know everything has a ripple effect. As it turned out, he got my card and he wanted a reading.

He came over to the flat, and said, 'Okay, so take out your cards.'

I said, 'I don't use cards.'

Although I know how to use cards, instead I tuned in and gave over the information that Spirit was giving me to tell him. Here's the point I want to make. The whole room, and I mean the whole room, was coloured in pink, it was a beautiful soft pink, the colour of the love we shared. It was amazing and I realised that nothing could take away the bond that had been created. We were the colour of love. It has had a spin-off effect with all the other reads I've ever done.

Emotions, intent, honesty, courage, love ... our souls bring everything with them into every room, every day, everywhere.

Before his brother went to New York to be mentored by an artist, he was playing at a venue in Melbourne. I decided to go and see him play. It was around this time that I was developing spiritually, although this development is ongoing. It was jazz and he is an incredible artist. The band was getting ready to play – a drummer, bass guitarist and Mark's brother Ben on keyboards. The crowd had gathered and were seated at tables as food and drink were being brought out in the upbeat restaurant. The soft sounds of the music filled the air and as I looked over at Ben I saw a light around him, a kind of golden light. At first I thought it was the lighting in the place but it was a late afternoon. I looked again and saw the same colour around him, a beautiful golden light. It was years later that I remembered this again as I started seeing more lights and auras around people.

Should you shield the canyons from the windstorms you would never see the true beauty of their carvings.
Elisabeth Kübler-Ross

The Princess cross

It was late August 1997, I was working at the government call centre and loved it. The job was busy – sometimes there were even 150 calls per day, but I thought I had it down pat. I was earning enough to pay rent and live as a single mother, which is a feat in itself. I had also made new friends and I enjoyed seeing them as part of my working week routine.

I felt it was important not to rush into working professionally as I wanted to be the best I could be before looking for professional work. I have since seen others jump into reading well before they have had enough experience. For me, in any case, it was a life journey.

Back to the story … It was a good 15-minute walk from the car park to the building that housed the call centre. It was pretty much like the movie *Groundhog Day* – same building, same desks, same supervisor, same questions – except that when I was walking in on this particular week something different was happening. As I looked over to see the desks or the people I was working with, even doors, there were dark crosses over them. The same thing happened that week even at the supermarket. I saw small black crosses to large black crosses. I'd see the crosses over random people walking down the street as I pulled up in my car to get out of it. The times or sequences between seeing them had no real pattern. Eventually I saw a black cross over a dear friend that I sat next to at the call centre. I had to say something, I couldn't hold back any longer and besides I was worried for her now. She knew I was a very spiritual person, so hopefully she wouldn't think I had lost my mind completely, so I mentioned it to her.

'I'm seeing black crosses, something's not right.'

She said, 'What?'

'I'm seeing black crosses.'

'What do you mean?' she said.

I replied, 'I'm seeing these black crosses, over people, over doors, down corridors.'

She said, 'Oh my God, Roni, I don't know but it sounds intense, mate … Oh my God, Roni, really? Oh my God!'

I was in my car on the day I heard the news Princess Diana was killed in a tragic car crash in the Pont de I'Alma road tunnel in Paris on 31 August 1997. It took my breath away to hear that news for a moment. I thought the news must be wrong, the kind of thing you think when you're in shock. I cried, not hysterical crying but shedding a tear for the People's Princess.

It was almost as if the tear spilling down my cheek had illuminated the memory of the week prior. It all made sense. The dark crosses I was seeing. The premonition. This was my sign for someone passing over. It can change but it was a sign. It also informed me of the connection that we all have as one.

Sign of the cross

While nursing one night a lovely lady had come to us from Emergency. She wasn't doing so well – she was in her late 70s, we had trouble feeding her and she wasn't tolerating swallowing her medications. We moved her to a high dependency unit, and we lovingly cleaned her and combed her hair. Something was drawing my eyes to look above her head and there I saw it again, the cross. It was huge and black, hanging above her.

The doctors were figuring out what was going on with her. Taken aback at what I saw, I asked the nurse in charge if I could ring the patient's daughter. The nurse thought it may have been too early – it was somewhat unclear as no tests had been done at the time. My instincts kept saying, 'ring the daughter'. The nurse in charge agreed that I could ring her. The daughter appreciated the phone call and I was aware of not too unduly worrying her but she wanted to come.

When she arrived there was still some ambiguity as to what was going on medically.

I motioned her daughter to be close, and my voice changed into the softest lull. I mentioned to her about following her gut instincts, and that the doctors would speak to her as soon as they could. She was worried about her mother's condition and asked if I thought it was serious. I knew it wasn't my call and that the doctors would be the best people to advise on her condition. We talked about her mother, how close they were and I encouraged her to be close to her, pulling up a seat just to hold her hand.

I kept the vision to myself.

Still as a professional, I asked the nurse in charge at the time if we had any palliative orders in place. She looked at me a bit startled. No, we hadn't initially, which is sometimes the case.

By the next day the patient's condition had deteriorated and she was diagnosed nil by mouth and weak. The daughter, Ivana, was happy to see me, and the team were not sure whether or not the patient would improve. The daughter asked me again what I thought. I wanted to tell her what I had seen but I knew it would scare her, and it wasn't my place. I kept the vision to myself.

'The doctors are investigating so I can't comment medically.' I also wasn't about to worry her daughter either, she had enough going on.

She replied with, 'Ronda, you can tell me what you think.'

I said, 'We only get one Mum,' as she held her mother's hand.

Ivana asked, 'How long have you been nursing?'

I replied, 'About nine years.'

We also spoke about life and faith. She was an only daughter and she recalled when she and her parents had come to Australia from Bosnia. They had fled when the war was on. She asked me where I grew up and I told her when I was little it was in a funeral parlour and that when my time came I wasn't afraid to pass as I believed in an afterlife. I didn't go into details as it wasn't professional to do so. She grabbed her mum's hand a little more strongly.

'Do you think Mum will make it through?'

Of course, we couldn't comment on diagnoses but at that stage it wasn't medically determined what was really happening.

I was working the following day and again had a chance to speak with Ivana. The doctors thought that Maria, her mother, had had a stroke. Ivana was by her side. We spoke of spiritual things from a faith perspective. Her Mum wasn't able to speak but she knew that Ivana was there beside her.

Ivana asked me, 'Ronda, why is your faith so strong when there is so much that is wrong in our world?' I told her the story of sensing my friend's father in the back seat of the car around the time he died.

She glanced over at her mother. 'That's incredible, Ronda.'

I said, 'Well, it made me think that there is more to life than we know and that we should be open-minded, and that we all have a journey. We are homeward bound to God from the time we arrive here.'

She kissed her mum on the cheek and soon afterwards left for the night. I wasn't on the next morning, because I was rostered on in the afternoon a day later. When I got in around 1.30pm, Maria had already died.

It was a couple of days later in the afternoon at the hospital when the nurse in charge called me to come to the front desk, as I had a visitor.

It was Ivana and her husband.

I said, 'Oh Ivana, I'm so sorry to hear about your mum.'

'Ronda, I came in to see you to thank you. The night that I left here when you were rostered on I had a dream. I dreamt that there was a terrible train crash and an uncle of mine from Bosnia, Zoran, walked out of the train. My uncle died years before, Ronda, but I knew that it was a sign. I knew then that Mum was going to pass over. I felt it in my heart and believed that he visited me to let me know. He was Mum's brother.

'So I said to my husband I'm going in to the hospital – it was around 3.30am in the morning when I had the dream. I got to the hospital later that morning. Mum wasn't palliated but I just knew it. She passed around 2pm in the afternoon.'

We were both crying, along with her husband. She was right – her mother had not yet been palliated.

She went on to say, 'I don't know how to thank you for all you said. When I woke up after the dream, I thought of you and I knew I had to see Mum early. Ronda, I could hardly speak, the tears were flowing down my face.'

She was thanking me for encouraging her to be free to follow her gut. It was because of this dream or premonition that she was able to say goodbye to her mother, in those last precious hours.

Spirits have a way of coming through sometimes when we least expect. It's like they know the storyline and outcome. Perhaps I saw the cross so vividly because the spirit world knew me and that I would be sensitive with Ivana; and that she would listen to the spirituality of seeing her uncle in the dream. At least they were going to try.

Working in palliative care is different as we can get ready to support a family and carers with the inevitable outcome of a passing. Losing someone quickly in a hospital setting can be distressing and cause shock emotionally for loved ones. Ivana had the chance to be lovingly at her mother's side as she passed. Her mother couldn't speak for herself or send a text to ask her daughter to come to the hospital. Yet somehow the universe through love was able to send a message to Ivana and she listened, with her heart.

Signs and symbols

I vividly remember the first symbol I was given by Spirit in a reading – it was during group work and it was my first official read. I was shown a pot of tea, not just an ordinary pot – it was red, green and gold, very Oriental looking. I knew what this meant, I said something along the lines of looking after your health, that was my symbol. It didn't mean they should go and have a cup of oriental tea.

The black cross sign wasn't something I was expecting to see and now during a reading I may or may not be given that sign to represent a passing. I may be given another; I may see a shadow or spirit behind the person sitting for a reading in a colour that I know how to interpret. We will all be given different signs depending on what our spirit guides give us. Over the years the signs and symbols that I've learnt to interpret have changed as I've evolved in my readings.

Once while I was driving to see some friends, in my mind I saw their house covered in red. Now at the time of seeing the image of their house in my mind, I interpreted that they must have had a fight or argument.

On arrival, the husband was at home and I was kindly ushered in. We struck up a conversation and I asked whether or not they had an argument prior to my arrival. I was still developing and they knew I was psychic, having known me since a teenager. His reply was no.

'Oh,' I said. 'This is so bizarre. On the drive over here I saw your whole house covered in red and I just felt you must have had an argument.'

He replied with a chuckle, 'Well, actually yes, we did have a bad argument.'

My signs for an argument in a relationship are varied. I may hear, see or feel as I'm giving over the information as a conduit between the person who is sitting for a reading and information coming from the spirit world. The important thing is to trust what you're given. It's also why I advocate that students take their time developing. It's as wonderful a journey developing psychic abilities as it is in using and reading for people. It's important to be honest with yourself. Had I not been honest in the last scenario with the house covered in red, I would have lost out in developing faith in my own ability.

Sometimes spirit guides are quite vocal in what they want to pass through to the living. I think I had probably been reading for eight or so years when I heard my guide say, 'Your sister's car is going to catch on fire, you need to let her know.'

Mmm, I wasn't doubting what I heard but I doubted severely whether or not my sister would take me seriously.

Regardless, I got on the phone, yes pre-mobiles, and rang. 'Um, Coral, I'm getting a message from my guide that your car is going to catch on fire.'

Her initial response was to laugh.

'Coral, I'm not joking, that's what she's telling me. I have to tell you because I don't want you to be hurt.'

I think she thought I was out there with the fairies. It was pretty far-fetched ... a car going to be on fire.

'Coral, that's what I'm being told.'

She replied, 'Roni, I don't know what to say.'

'I have to tell you, though, the feeling is so strong.'

'Roni, I just don't know what to think of this, it's bizarre.'

'Yes, I know it's strange but I have to say it like it is. I'm being told the car is going to catch on fire.'

I put the phone down knowing what she thought but I had done my job. I trusted and that was the important part. I had faith in the message I was given. I had relayed that message over to the right person and although it was ahead of time (clairvoyantly) I had done my best. Even though I think my sister thought I was a complete nutcase.

Approximately three weeks later her purple Ford Escort caught on fire and her partner and his friend were in the car. Having jumped out in shock, they apparently hid behind a tree and a guy got out a hose to hose it down. The fire brigade also arrived. It was in Windsor, a busy suburb of Melbourne.

We talk about that story to this day. To me it's a testament of trust in what's being given to you. Signs can be visual or they can also be clairaudiently given.

I was driving home one night when I heard the word 'shock'. Um okay. I was still in the car when I heard the word again – shock. Okay, I wasn't sure what it meant as I was driving, then I heard it again – shock.

When I got back to the flat I turned on the answering machine as by that time I was ready for some sort of news. I was ready for the shock that Spirit was warning me of. I went into my bedroom and then I saw it – the biggest spider I have ever seen in my life. I think they are called bird spiders. Yes, they were right yet again. I got a shock alright and was so glad that my daughter wasn't at home for the night. I went to a 7/11 and got some spray. I don't know where it hid. It was another confirmation I was learning and I was developing, grateful and humbled by every experience.

Signs and symbols are great tools for psychics and mediums to decipher information. It's important to remember, though, that we are all different in the way that we work. The modality you are strongest in will affect the type of messages that you receive as symbols. For example, if you are predominantly clairvoyant and see things, your symbols may be more visual. Along with that, we use our minds to interpret the symbols and signs and we need to be able to unravel what we subconsciously pick up.

If someone is clairsentient – that is, using the 'sense of feeling' – they also need to unravel that feeling that they are subconsciously picking up on. They may be feeling an emotion like sadness but will need to also relay where that fits – is it connected to a romance, a passing or something else? This comes with practice and being open and in tune.

Butterfly sister

Spirit give us signs and symbols all the time but are we listening? Are we in tune?

My sister Leigh passed away on grand final day 2010. I had visited her the night before, and she had told me she was going out with a friend the following day. I remember thinking of her the day she passed, and I should have gone over to see her. I had another engagement to attend. She had told me she was going out but yet I kept thinking of her. There was a light around her on the night before she passed, but I didn't think of it connected to her dying. She was psychic too, very much so. Her life was centred round her two girls whom she adored more than anything in the world. She was supersensitive. She was always for those who had a struggle, she was for the underdog, she was intelligent, intellectual, my best friend and confidante. I couldn't believe I didn't see her passing coming. We can't see everything, and sometimes we are not supposed to know. I'd lost my soul sister – I remained alive but I felt half dead.

It was around 8 o'clock at night that my daughter and I got the call. I remember just beforehand I was lying on the bed with the cat cuddled up next to me. I remember feeling as if I were falling under water. (She was found under water.) Then my daughter gave me the news. I screamed so loudly. I just screamed and screamed and screamed. No … not my sister, no.

We did the funeral like people do funerals, with the flowers, the speeches, the songs. I felt hollow, and her children lost their mother – her laughter, her vision of thought, her sensitivity. She got it, she was on my side, we were the single mums in the family, we understood the struggle to survive, the cutbacks. I was nursing and I understood her struggle as a mother, financially and emotionally. Now … I just missed her, we all did. She was the salt of the earth in our family. Sometimes misrepresented, sometimes misunderstood.

I asked a love interest if he would come with me on the day of her funeral. He agreed. I will always be grateful that he came with me. Friends and family gathered and some of Mum's friends even flew from Canberra to attend. It was October and the sun had come out before a crowd gathered to go into the chapel. John stood behind me and a girlfriend of mine was in view. I thought it was funny she didn't come over to say hello but just stood there. Then one of the most intense auras I have ever seen came into view. Suddenly, without warning, just before going into the chapel I saw the colour green surround my friend. It was as green as green and thick and dense and spread out about a foot and a half all the way around her body.

How funny – it was just as she was looking over at me and the guy standing behind me. Sadly, I felt the aura reflected jealousy and, funnily enough, after the service she proceeded to make sure he knew how old I was because he was a few years younger than me, which he wasn't aware of at the time and she knew that. Another confirmation. Along with seeing the green I could feel her envy. I understand now the phrase 'green with envy'. I was still shocked nonetheless, especially as this happened on the day of my sister's funeral.

Perhaps my sister was there, protecting me, showing me something I hadn't seen before. It was another incredible moment as I saw what I saw as my heart was breaking.

After the funeral we drove to the family home where we gathered. The friend who had accompanied me to the service drove back with me. Family and friends were at the house, although it wasn't much of a 'wake'; it was too sad, just a flat feeling accompanied by a sense that she really should still be with all of us.

I walked back to the car and noticed the headlights were on. I hadn't noticed the lights on when I pulled up. I felt it was her presence.

A few months later I was babysitting her children. It was so raw; her not being there and the suffering they endured ripped my heart apart.

As I left them, I returned back to my car in broad daylight. The headlights were on. Again, I never had them on to drive over. Again, I just thought of her ...

I went back to work too early – I never had enough time out to really grieve properly. Friends came and went showing their compassion and sympathy.

It was about a year later that I dreamt of her – it was so vivid. I was staying with a friend who is also a psychic medium.

In my dream I had walked into a flat and I could smell incense burning. I noticed floorboards in a room somewhere, and then I saw her face. I felt the shock and joy of seeing her. Her eyes were red, and I knew it was a sense of her sadness of not being with her girls here on this side. We spoke but not with words. She wanted me to know that she was safe on the other side and that she was learning now about her time spent here. We spoke by just looking at each other and we cried, too. We were communicating telepathically and my heart was all there with her. She showed me a ring for a relationship that I would find and an overseas holiday after my mother passed. My mother is still alive. I was told to read more. I woke up with tears streaming down my face. I couldn't get back to sleep for ages. In the morning, I told my friend and just cried again. My friend agreed it was a psychic dream where my sister had visited.

We communicated through our eyes and I knew she missed being here and the love we shared as much as I missed having her here to share the laughter and conversations as sisters do. It felt eternal, our bond – it felt as if she would always somehow be there for me on another level. I wouldn't have her physical presence in the way I always had but she would be ever present with me in another way.

She showed herself as slightly younger, and the vibration of humility and sensitivity was there as she had it here on earth. I was so touched that she came through. It woke me up and I remember crying in my dream as we spoke, only to wake up with tears running down my cheek.

I was thinking of her around the time of her birthday – it was a year after she passed. I was sad that she wasn't here to celebrate and see how well her daughters were doing. I missed her so much. I was on afternoon duty so had decided to go for a coffee at my local shopping mall. It is enclosed by large glass doors with many shops, coffee shops, Coles and an area where you can buy a coffee and just sit down and enjoy it. I ordered a mocha and sat down on a comfy black sofa. While I was sitting down enjoying the coffee, a butterfly touched my elbow. *Oh wow*, I thought, *a butterfly actually touching my elbow*. I could feel the delicate brush of its wing like an eyelash against my skin. Then I realised that only half an hour or so ago, I was thinking about her. She was here with me in spirit. She was the butterfly or sending the butterfly but she was here with me in spirit.

I had saved up enough money to see one of my favourite mediums in the world, Lisa Williams, and I had told a friend who was also a medium about her workshops in Australia. We were really excited to see her and hear her speak.

She was awesome and we learnt from one of the best. During her platform workshop I looked over at one of the students and I saw my sister's face, over her face.

It was a busy day, we were all having a go at platform and it was the last thing I was expecting. The energy in the room was electric and I put the vision down to the increased energy of the room. I was blown away that I had seen her face. Later that evening, Lisa was on stage doing what she does best, bringing through messages from the other side. As I was sitting watching her deliverance, it happened again. I saw Lisa's face change into Leigh's face. The highlight for me was seeing my sister's face – such a cosmic experience.

The next day at the airport, I rang my daughter, as I was travelling back to Melbourne. 'Darling, it was amazing, I saw Leigh's face twice on the same day and that night while Lisa was on stage.'

Then my daughter interrupted and said, 'Mum, last night the fan just came on by itself in your room.'

Last night was when I saw her face … We both started crying. At the airport I must have looked so strange. They were tears of happiness and joy. Leigh was with us and she was so clever.

I also remembered the dream at my friend's house. You need to read more was the impression I was given from her. I worked out why … because I would be writing …

As I look back now, I think of the fan that came on when I saw her image interstate, the butterfly in the shopping mall and the headlights being on the day of the funeral and later when babysitting her children. I think of seeing the image of the aura around my friend at the service and of seeing and communicating with her in a dream. All of those signs.

We are speaking the language of Spirit without words, and when the heart is in the right place, we see everything. Everything that needs to be seen, heard and felt in an instance. Through the eyes of love, the heart and soul resound and connect us to those we love. Time and space penetrable, easily, eternally.

She had visited me.

Angels

When my daughter and I were living in the share house we struggled, and there were days when I had little money left to go around. Being a single mother has taught me many things but mostly resilience.

This was a typical day for me, I had picked up my daughter from school and we were on our way out. I never had a new car until I was in my forties and the car I had at the time was reasonable but it needed work every now and then. The mechanics of the car wasn't the problem.

We ran out of petrol on the train lines in a busy area of suburban Melbourne. Exactly on the train lines at around 4.30pm. When it happened, I think my heart fell directly into a pit in my stomach.

I said to my daughter, 'Get ready to jump!'

I was pumping the accelerator but the empty red light just flashed. At that point I got out of the car. The intersection was on a stretch of road that was quite even. I looked behind me and saw at least forty cars stretching into the distance. One guy had got out of his car, arms outstretched in rage as if to imply 'what's the hold-up?'

I got back inside to tell her to jump out. As I got inside, the car moved slowly off the rails.

We were safe. You could say that the motion of getting out of the car that day helped to move the vehicle. It has to this day always amazed me, however, as the area was flattish and the car had stopped dead on the tracks. The road at Tooronga Station actually inclines upwards towards Hawthorn, which was the direction we were travelling. So it's still amazing. No one got out of their cars to help or if they did I never heard or saw them, just the angry guy at the back of the built-up line of traffic.

I felt we had a guardian angel that day – it always springs to mind when people speak of angels. It wasn't our time.

Doorway

This next story takes me to the hospital once again. For sensitivity reasons, I won't go into the details and situation. I can say this though: the day the patient passed I was working, and I had looked after this patient many times. We got to know and care for our patients, as some become like family after looking after them for long periods of time. It's difficult to see them deteriorate. When this patient's condition became more serious, we all went into limbo-land.

While working one afternoon as the patient became more unwell, I could see a light behind the patient's mother. As she was walking onto the ward one afternoon, I heard a name starting with N; it sounded like Norma or Nora, who I found out later was the patient's grandmother who had passed on. I also saw a light around the mother of the patient when I heard the name.

We all knew the inevitable was coming. It got to the stage where it became difficult to see Chippie (their nickname) knowing they weren't doing well and knowing that they were clinging on with frailty while those loved ones stayed as close as possible to be there and wait.

It was during the day and I went to sit in another room to have a cuppa as the family were at the bedside. No one else was in the room. Well, I should rephrase that: no one from this side was in the room. When I looked over opposite me, I could see a shadow building up and I felt a great grandparent was there. They were waiting along with others to collect the patient and they would not be alone on the other side.

They in spirit had been collecting for weeks and hovering near, getting ready to rejoice with the spirit that would be returning home. But on this side the pain was intolerable and heavy going.

They were waiting.

Then I saw to the left of me the brightest white light ever imaginable, whiter than white just flash in very quickly, and I heard a strong powerful voice say, 'Not much longer.'

I knew it wouldn't be long.

Chippie passed approximately 20 minutes later. I could almost feel a sense of departure. I was back on the ward and there seemed to me a different kind of feeling, as if there had been a drop in temperature or a silence and softening in the atmosphere.

They had boarded that flight to spirit. Their time was nigh and yet here on this side time seemed to stand still as if there were no sense of time at all.

The spirit world knew, and they were doing their job to greet on the other side. The grace I felt that night and the humility was incredible – the sense as well that we are the miracle, life itself, time itself that we reside in.

We couldn't believe this patient had left, even though we expected it. My heart hung heavily for the loss but I also felt as if I had glimpsed a slice of heaven and I felt peaceful that they would no longer be suffering. It's hard for those left behind.

That night left me feeling that there are angels and a higher realm as I recalled seeing the light, as well as the powerful voice.

One can ask so many questions at this point. How does Spirit know? How many of those in spirit were collecting close by? Why didn't anyone else pick up on the sensation?

It lends itself to thinking about many things. The healing quality of love, the circle of life and the compassion that both sides of life here on the earthly realm and the other side are composed of. I started to think about my mother and her near death experience and seeing a white light.

I thought about how a family ache for a loved one, to just hold them one more time and kiss them one last time. The sense that gone forever brings. How people can leave so suddenly or linger in pain.

'To companion so not as to fix but rather to assist the other in enlightenment or to open a window of hope for survival of the soul in the everlasting light of the universe.'[2]

There is a struggle that we here have with loss and grief, the world we live in and the way that we view death and the soul and our faith and where that leads us in our theology. Yet it boils down to connections and the power of love, the bond that we have with those closest to us and what we learn and continue to learn from them long after they are gone.

I had become the other in the room, like a bird that had just flown in to witness the suffering, with head bowed giving reverence to the life that they had led.

I thought about how death brings humility, how it's a leveller. Being able to see oneself in life's tapestry and the part we play. Making sense of deeper meanings and our beliefs and faith traditions and how they support us during the hard times. Scenes shot into my heart, piercing the life force that can be so fragile, shattering like pieces of glass that would never be the same only to reveal no barrier and a likeness that hurts for the other, a oneness, a humanity and love at the core of being in service. To acknowledge the sacred eternal in ourselves communicating with the sacred eternal in another soul …

A verse I wrote sums this up for me –

Mercy resides in this room
Tubes in a body so thin and shadows fill spaces
Love lights the room
It enters where there is such sorrow
Love holds the space
Where there has been shallow
Love keeps the memories
Of time.

Albert Schweitzer published an article 'The ethics of reverence for life' in the periodical *Christendom*.[3] He tells of a story of a gardener in

---

[2] Rumbold, B. *Spirituality and palliative care, social and pastoral perspectives*, Melbourne, Oxford University Press, 2002, p. 198

[3] Schweitzer, A, 'The ethics of reverence for life' in *Christendom*, vol 1, 1936, pp. 225-39

Scotland who captured one bird from a flock of geese and clipped its wings before releasing it. The rest of the flock flew away but noticed that the other bird could not fly properly though it tried. The flock observed this and settled back onto the pond and waited for days until the injured bird was healed enough to resume flight with the flock. This is nature informing us of the care of the other, gifting us into the reverence we can have for the other.

I hope one day when I pass that my soul is able to fly around those I love, to watch over them and have a bird's eye view, to be so close when they are going through trials and troubles and the world seems like a harsh place. I hope I can be like a bird and sit on their windowsill or gaze from a distance, in sight, silently but ever present with loving eyes always close by. If a tear falls, I can fly by and with the wing of a bird's feather, catch it and send it to heaven.

As we begin to know that our spirit is eternal, we know love is eternal. In the miracle that we witness in the spirit communicating from discarnate to incarnate, we recognise love communicating. We recognise a bridge to which eternity can be crossed back and forth.

As we call to our soul when we are wishing to speak and see those we love, we are reminded that the great spirit where they reside is with us all the time. For each and every one of us lives eternally and the communication between the two worlds is in harmony. As the birds know, that fly high above us. And as the great source of intelligence the spirit world gifts us with knows. Love doesn't die, it is eternal.

Echo

It was a privilege to work as a nurse in palliative care with patients and their families, and I learned much from that experience. As a trainee pastoral care practitioner, being there for a patient in their last earthly hours was such an honor. It's hard to put into words the deep reverence I felt sitting in a chair next to a dying lady who was lucid enough to hear me.

'I can see that it is a sunny day outside and the wind is gently blowing through the leaves on a tree just near the window. The birds are chirping and soon leaves will start to fall.'

She took in a deep breath as tubes were attached to her to assist her breathing and there was a distinct smile etched on her face. I looked over at her lovingly and knew she would soon be gone. Yet there was something almost poignant about the light gently caressing the room and its dappled pattern reflected on the wall opposite the bed. I can understand why many wished her to stay. She left in autumn, and in spring there would be new fresh buds on the blossom branches.

As we cross over, we are reborn into the matter of being what we truly are ... as nature would have it so ... programmed to be souls ... wired to God ... to infinity ...

The birthday party

An 18th birthday party is a big deal, no matter who or where you are. This one was nonetheless in the outer suburbs of Melbourne on a spring night. I had arrived early to assist with getting it all together. There was the usual hum associated with excitement and joy. The house had been decorated well and a DJ with music were dedicated to a space outside where partygoers could dance and hang out. The house had a wall that was filled with photos and there was food everywhere and large containers with alcohol.

Jemma looked like a princess with her black shoulder-length hair and blue eyes. Most of the people at the party were well dressed, with the girls in short colourful outfits and the boys neat and tidy. It was a privilege to be there. I assigned myself to be security on the door as the guests arrived. Some arrived in pairs, some as couples. Some arrived in groups as I ticked their names off the guest list. Some arrived with alcohol and permission letters from parents.

I was so impressed with the behaviour of all who attended. The parents would have been so proud as everyone was so responsible and socialised well with each other. There was a lovely warmth about the presence of everyone on the night. I kept myself busy by sorting out some of the food to take on platters outside. Wine flowed as we enjoyed champagne for the special evening.

Music sounded and you could hear the sound of voices all meshed together as a frequency around the house and no doubt outside of the premises where the neighbours knew of the occasion. Cars packed the street and there would have been little room for anyone else as the house was full. The food was delicious and well planned with the cake hidden neatly away as we kept on taking food outside while it was hot on plates.

Then as the evening wore on it came time for the speeches. The first speaker was a school friend of Jemma's. You could hear a hush as the noise of the crowd simmered down to a volume that buzzed softly until there was a space of silence that my ears quickly absorbed as tender and soothing. She spoke so well and I stood back with a bird's eye view from the kitchen looking over at the scene where a marquee was erected.

When she finished her speech, it was Jemma's mother's turn to speak. I smiled as I observed the love she had and the stories she shared of Jemma growing up in the country and of the family running a bed and breakfast business while she was a toddler. They were a hard-working Aussie family bringing up the kids and working together to make ends meet. Jemma smiled as the speech was beautifully done and the bond between them was easily felt in the crowd.

Then it was Jemma's turn to speak. She confidently took centre stage as the crowd eagerly awaited her response. She'd worked really hard and had already achieved great results academically. It was about then I began to sense a male trying to get my attention but not anyone who was at the party, a male in spirit. I began to feel something in my head as if I had a headache when I didn't have a headache. Then as I looked over at Jemma I could see an image starting to appear of a man standing next to her. It didn't come into full view yet I sensed it was a man standing there. He was showing me that something had happened to his leg, that he had been in a kind of accident. I could also see a station wagon that he had. I knew it was someone in the spirit world wanting to let her know that he was around for her birthday. Along with the feelings that someone was there and the vision being imprinted on me through the third eye, I also felt that it was her father.

I didn't want to say anything initially but later on, I let her mother know. She knew that I was a medium. I told her what I saw that night.

She told me he did have something wrong with his leg, he had climbed onto the roof of the house at one point and jumped off, injuring it. He had also regularly complained of a varicose vein in the leg as well. And yes, he did have a station wagon – it was the first car they had bought when Jemma was born.

The message had got through to Jemma and tears were shed.

It was the natural cosmic laws of the universe, gifting his presence.

Do you see what I see?

We are all psychic. There may be times when you're thinking of someone you haven't heard from in a while and then they ring or text you from out of the blue. You may think that you really need to pump up the back tyre on your car and a day later, oops, you have a flat tyre. You may be driving and thinking it feels as if there is a police vehicle on the road today with a speed camera and, voila, you soon pass one. Then receive a speeding fine a week or so later.

Sometimes what can be difficult about being psychic is vibing into a family occurrence. Just before falling to sleep one night, I saw my daughter's black Hyundai Getz, spinning around. I knew that Spirit were showing me a future event, yet in the back of my mind I said to myself, 'Oh, perhaps I'm just imagining it.' I had been saying to my daughter for months that she probably needed a new car, as her drive to work had been longer as we had moved further out.

It came to pass that she had a car accident on her way to work and it wiped out her car. She mentioned that before the accident occurred, a rock hit her car from out of the blue. Yes, I was surprised when I heard that, too – a rock just out of nowhere, a small one, hit her windscreen and she slowed down in her vehicle.

She said, 'Mum, at that moment I was thinking of Grandpa.'

Shortly after that, a car hit her. She was off work for a couple of days with whiplash and a mighty headache but thankfully she was okay.

Trust what you're given. It was difficult for me to have seen the message and really I just wanted to change it. Being honest with yourself and others is important in a reading, as we all want the best and we all want to hear the best. Honesty is the best policy. The rock hitting the windscreen is still to us a miracle. Thanks, Grandpa.

Spirits show themselves at times when you are least expecting to see or hear from them. In order to do so, they slow their vibration down to make their presence felt. My friend Alice had lost her mother a few years before this incident. She and her father were enjoying a drink in the afternoon sun when I dropped over to see them. He naturally was still grappling with the idea of losing her. She had lived well into her 80s but as the partner who was left grieving, it wasn't easy for him and it was easy to see his pain and suffering at the loss of his beloved while in his presence. I sat down on a comfortable chair under a sail and while listening to the conversation and making a mental note of how he must have been feeling, I sensed my friend's mother standing next to her beloved partner. She was coming through and I could see a shadow that soon disappeared. I couldn't make out her features but I knew it was her.

It felt inappropriate to say anything, unethical in a way and I also sensed that he would feel quite flabbergasted even though he knew me. I guess it just didn't feel right at the time. It was the beginning of sensing and tuning into spirit in a newfound way. I sat for the rest of the time that afternoon dumbfounded and I don't think anything else in their conversation sunk in with me. I was still learning and although I had done thousands of readings (sometimes nine a day in the shop where I was working), at that point I wasn't sure if the timing was right to say anything. Love brings spirit closer. A whole range of emotions opened up and a new sense of philosophy was brewing but love was opening the veil to the world beyond ours. As my philosophy deepened, so too did my sense of what I was doing deepen. I preferred a session with them one on one in my own time. I was also getting into platform demonstrations in front of small audiences. Nursing kept me busy and was shift work so it was difficult at times to have the energy to do both.

Do you hear what I hear?

Kerani is a girl's name of Hindi origin, meaning 'sacred bells'.

Hearing with clairaudience can be confronting at times and it's important to be as honest and clear as possible in the interpretation for the sake of the person you are reading for with integrity, purity and truth.

One of my sisters and I would often discuss spiritual matters as she was very psychic herself and had a very intellectual spin on spiritual matters. It's not an uncommon fact that if a family member can do readings, members of the immediate family will request readings from time to time. The immediate family will often glean information on the spirit world from one who is a medium. I was lucky in that my family were very supportive and didn't make me feel as if I were crazy – it was quite the opposite, perhaps because of living in a funeral parlour as a child. Nonetheless.

On 6 September 2001, I called in to visit my sister and she really wanted a reading so I agreed. Various things came through for her and she was very happy. And then the message I received baffled us both.

'Something is about to happen and we are doing everything we can to stop them.'

My sister and I were taken aback, and for a second time the message came through.

'Something is about to happen and we are doing everything we can to stop them.'

'What do they mean, Roni?'

I said, 'Leigh, I don't know.'

We knew it didn't pertain to her or me but, again, we were baffled. After a cuppa or two, I made my way home.

Days later at around 11:30pm, the phone rang. It was so late that I was worried and jumped out of bed so as not to miss the call.

'Roni, it's Leigh, put the TV on.'

'What?'

'Roni, put the TV on, it's about the message that was coming through in the reading the other afternoon.'

'Okay.' I switched on the TV, having absolutely no idea of what I was about to see.

It was 9/11 and it was being televised in Australia. All I could see was smoke coming from buildings, mayhem, chaos and destruction, total and utter destruction …

I couldn't believe my eyes. At first I thought it must have been a bomb or something. It kept on going, it was filmed from America.

I sat motionless. 'Spirit were trying to do everything they could.' My heart broke.

So many innocent lives lost in such a senseless act of terror. It touched the very core of my being as we know the world watched and prayed for those lives lost. We prayed for the spirits of those who had left so suddenly and for their families. We in Australia, as all over the world, were hearing the stories of immense bravery and honour.

We felt a kinship to America and during that time I sensed the spirit of a young girl who had only recently started a job. I sensed the name Marion and lit a candle for her. I cried at the thought of losing a child in such a horrific way. The prayers of the living carrying those lost into the arms of angels.

God bless those that lost their lives so tragically that day. Into the arms of angels.

The whole is something greater than the sum of its parts.
Aristotle

Was it collective or universal consciousness gifting us the message? Was it the spirit world? I'm not entirely sure but it reminds me of the quote above. The 'whole' being greater, responding, emerging, invoking, awakening the part of the whole that we exist in, are a part of.

Conscious wave

It was 2004 and my daughter and I were living together. I was reading and still developing and working. I vividly remember being in the kitchen when I heard a large bell sound in my head, a kind of boom. At first I thought nothing of it, it was 20 December. I kept going about my business, cleaning and cooking. Later that day it happened again, that 'boom' and a kind of rush and low, low vibration. I knew it was different from anything that I'd ever experienced before but I couldn't explain it. There was a sound, there was a feeling.

The next day it happened again with an almost bell-like ring with the 'boom'.

I said to my daughter, 'Something's about to happen, like an enormous explosion, one of the worst the world has ever seen, like a volcano, a massive occurence.'

My daughter turned around as I said these words.

'I've been hearing this sound, honey. I just can't explain it, but it's going to be big, really massive.'

For that entire week I would hear the thud sound, and then a kind of bell ring in my head. I knew something was going to hit and it was going to be huge.

The 2004 Indian Ocean Earthquake occurred on 26 December 2004. The resulting tsunami killed around 230,000 people in 14 countries, with waves up to 30 metres high. It was one of the deadliest natural disasters on record. The earthquake was a magnitude of 9.1-9.3. Apparently the entire planet actually vibrated by 1cm, triggering earthquakes as far away as Alaska. The tsunami caused damage and deaths reaching as far as the east coast of Africa. States of emergency were raised in Sri Lanka, Indonesia and the Maldives.

Our hearts hung in sorrow for the tumultuous loss. An apocalyptic event. I will never forget what I heard beforehand. As I write it now, I imagine I wasn't the only one. Millions of psychics across the globe will have their stories. We are all connected and connected to the earth, to Mother Earth and her precious, most precious children.

Did people hear sounds like that before Mount Vesuvius exploded in 79 AD and buried the ancient city of Pompeii? Are we listening? Are we listening with our hearts?

Love each other.

Darren's story

I met Darren in Melbourne when we worked at a busy call centre for three years, day after day. As with many colleagues at work, we got to know each other well and shared the same views on spiritual matters and beliefs. With his permission and much honour and respect, I have included two of his stories as I felt they are so precious and give an insight to the world of Spirit. The following story is in his own words and the one that follows has been written for him after taking notes and receiving the details.

The wedding

In the autumn of 1999, my Uncle Graeme passed away after a long battle with stage 4 melanoma, leaving behind my four cousins who were young adults with a future ahead that now their father could no longer be a part of.

Personally, I have always believed that death is a transition to the other side and while those we love are no longer in this physical world, they remain with us always. If we have an open heart and open mind and listen to our inner self, they can and will make their presence known.

Like every little girl, my cousin Kerry dreamt of her wedding day, the day that would be filled with lots of happy memories, and like every other girl imagined her dad there right by her side on her special day. In the months leading up to the wedding, Kerry confided that she wished more than anything that somehow and in some way her dad could be there with her.

I was close to Kerry and our family connection was strong, based on some previous experiences. I assured her that her dad would definitely be there on her special day. I encouraged Kerry to put it out there into the universe, with her heart and mind open to a sign from her dad. Just look and listen, he will send you a sign and you will know, without doubt, he will make his presence known.

The big day finally arrived. It was a typical spring day in Melbourne in 2005 and the weather was perfect, around 26 degrees with just a little cloud cover. As the guests arrived, they just couldn't believe what a beautiful day it was. The church was a 150-year-old bluestone church, very traditional with stunning lead lighting and a magnificent aisle marked by a red carpet that led to the altar where Kerry was to be married.

The bride arrived and looked stunning as she stepped out of the car, veil in check and her long train flowing behind. Inside the church as the music played, Kerry's proud brother walked her slowly down the aisle. Kerry beamed as she walked step by step, looking around and smiling as she continued down the aisle.

As the priest commenced the ceremony he asked, 'Who gives this woman to be married?'

A stream of sunlight appeared and shone through Kerry's veil, not around anyone else. I smiled to myself as I knew this was my uncle letting her know that he was there looking over her. Kerry also realised and, as we briefly caught each other's eye, Kerry gave me a big smile, seeming to acknowledge that she knew her dad was with her.

There were hymns sung, verses read and finally Kerry was now a married woman. She walked back up the aisle, outside to the gathering crowd awaiting to shower the newlyweds with confetti and congratulations. I had snuck out a little earlier so I could capture the happy couple walking out of the church and photograph them.

As you walk out of the church, you walk out into a magnificent garden surrounded by trees. To your left and right there are two pathways – one leads to the street, the other to a place where photos can be taken. There is a rose garden directly behind an old park bench in the shade of a large oak tree. Guests were busy taking pictures and greeting the new couple as they do at weddings, when all of a sudden out the corner of my eye I noticed a gentleman who had not been in the church attending the wedding. He stood back just near the bench and was dressed as you would expect any father of the bride to be. He wore a charcoal suit that included a yellow rose tucked into his lapel.

I briefly glanced over to take a closer look, and there was my uncle, beaming, looking at his little girl now married to the man of her dreams. My uncle looked healthy, as I remembered him before he fell ill. Excited, I turned to look at Kerry, then as quickly as he appeared, he had disappeared.

Later that night at the reception, I walked over to Kerry. We took hold of each other's hands and looked into each other's eyes. Kerry's eyes welled with happy tears and she smiled from ear to ear as she leaned in and gave me a big hug.

She whispered, 'He made it, like you said he would! My day could not have been any better!'

Tasha

Darren called Tasha his cousin and, though they were not blood-related, his mother looked after Tasha as a toddler, so they were close-knit. They had a great and deep connection growing up, and shared each other's company.

Darren was turning 40 and was planning a birthday party to celebrate the occasion. His own father had not long passed away and Tasha was at the funeral. Darren immediately sensed something wasn't right and was emphatic about that. He had a gut feeling for about 18 months prior to the funeral but they had drifted apart a little.

Darren left a message on Tasha's answering machine to let her know about the party and wondered whether or not she would come. Most people got back to him but Tasha didn't. He felt a sense of urgency to contact her.

Just before his birthday, Darren had a day of feeling completely restless and was unable to concentrate on anything at work during the day. He said his mind just wasn't on the job. He had a headache, felt confused and constricted the whole day. His friends even mentioned that he 'wasn't himself'. He also had a pain in his neck during the day, on and off.

Later that night, his aunty rang and told him the news. 'Tasha has hung herself.'

At first, he couldn't believe it. He was stunned and shocked. He stated that after 7pm that night he had felt better somehow and was advised by his aunty that this was around the time she had passed.

In Darren's heart and soul, he asked Tasha for a sign to let him know that she was okay.

Tasha was a huge fan of the *Rocky Horror Show*. She used to dress up in fishnet stockings and go the whole look for a night out for the screening at the Valhalla Cinema in Richmond, Melbourne. They would go many times together. She was a bit of a wild child and a free spirit. On the night she passed, Darren had to go and pick up his partner at a nightclub. He was still raw from the news and aware that he had asked her for a sign as he walked into the nightclub. The theme from the *Rocky Horror Show* was blaring through the speakers.

He was invited to the funeral home for the viewing but as he approached the premises, a branch fell from a tree and crossed his path before entering. He took this as a sign to remember his beloved friend the way she was.

Tasha, you live on in Spirit. For Darren he felt, apart from the devastation that somehow, somewhere her spirit had moved to a place free of pain and suffering. Together they will dance the Time Warp when his time comes, but for now she lives in his heart and soul. He tells me also of a picture that was taken of her on the beach that has become a precious relic in his house. He says he always knew she would leave early, she was so free and untameable.

Time and love are so precious.

Ken's story

We acknowledge the traditional owners of country throughout Australia and recognise their continuing connection to land, waters and culture. We pay our respects to their elders past, present and emerging.

A good friend of mine works with artists and says that it never really feels like work as he loves it so much. He had travelled to the Western Desert in the Northern Territory where he and a group had set up camp. Busy during the day exploring the terrain, they had a meal over a campfire and then rested in their swags as the embers burned down.

He was awoken in the middle of the night by the sound of what he said was 'women singing'. It woke him up and he listened for a good ten minutes or so and swallowed some water as he did. He thought it was one of the women in the group, Glenys, who had gathered together some of the black and white women to sing so beautifully.

In the morning he went over to the ladies' camping area. He thought Glenys was 'a sweetheart', and that the singing was 'such a lovely thing to do'. He remarked to her that he had enjoyed the singing that night.

Glenys had replied that it wasn't anyone in the group singing in the night but they had all heard it, too.

When the Indigenous people in the group heard the story, they said, 'Oh, that's the ancestors.'

They knew what it was straightaway. My friend went down to the waterhole nearby where the music had been emanating from overnight. He was looking for footprints and signs of life. He found none. The ancestors were singing for them, perhaps keeping them safe from harm as well. It is something he will never forget.

Della's story

Della and her mother had heard about my readings through some friends and they were referred on. I prepared for the readings in my usual way, being reverent of the gift and making time to relax and build the power through prayer and meditation. They had their readings separately and then together to see if Spirit had any further messages for them.

A grandfather came through showing himself as a strong patriarchal protector saying he 'was around them, protecting them.'

He also showed he was standing in front of a large gate at Della's house, which was confirmed.

As they were leaving, I also gave them some holy oil of Mary, which I had been given from a family in Melbourne who had a miraculous occurrence of oil coming from a statue. Many would travel to pray and see the miracle and receive the oil. I had kept sachets of it and gave some away. They were very grateful and we said our goodbyes.

Later that afternoon I received a voicemail message to call them back, and that they were anxious to speak with me. I did so and they told me what happened as they were driving home.

They were driving and talking about the experience of the readings, swapping information here and there and then they spoke of the grandfather's spirit coming through and the way that he was still protecting them. At that very instant, Della reported that an earring, a stud earring, popped out of her ear but with the backing intact. They took it as a sign.

She couldn't explain how the earring could have just popped so suddenly onto her lap intact, and they felt it was the grandfather adding credence to his presence in spirit. Perhaps the holy oil, too, had created a sacrosanct atmosphere. As they say, readings are stronger on holy ground.

Della was happy to share the story and they were excited to call me back in the afternoon to let me know what had transpired. She felt it would be a gift to share the story.

Time

I have heard stories like this one on many occasions. A granddaughter and her grandmother were close, sharing that special bond that we all know too well. The grandmother had fallen sick and her granddaughter was devastated. She had a strange feeling on the night that her grandma passed away and she rang her mother early the next day.

Her feelings proved to be correct – yes, her grandmother had passed away. She felt a kind of stunned feeling and shock that she wasn't able to be with her, at her bedside at that very special moment when the soul leaves the body and returns to Spirit.

She was so sad. She asked her mother when her grandma had passed, at what time. Her mother then told her it was 4.35am. She soon finished the conversation, letting her mother know she would be over at some stage to see her and, with that, the conversation over the phone ceased.

She was at home in that kind of fuzzy feeling you have when people pass, a feeling that reminds us we are not immortal and one day we will all return to source. We are reminded that time is precious and it's important to remind those we are close to that we love them, so that they are aware. We can notice the wind in the breeze and take notice of the simple things that nature offers, such as a butterfly or the leaves on the tree just outside. This granddaughter was in that kind of mood as the phone went down: sad, retrospective about the special relationship that we share with our grandparents and how empty we feel when they pass over, knowing we won't see them in the flesh like we once did, wondering and reminiscing over those wonderful moments we've had with them that we will cherish forevermore.

She then glanced down at her watch. It had stopped at 4.35am, the exact time that her grandma had passed.

She wasn't with her grandmother when she passed but with physical mediumship things can move and love can speak without words through time and space. Although the body itself is not immortal, the love that a grandmother had for her grandchild was able to transcend time and space and leave an indelible mark on her heart that she would keep safe in the knowledge that her love was less than a second away.

Robert J's story

Robert is a medium who has been working in Melbourne for many, many years. He has taught and organised fairs and is respected within the spiritual community for his sensitivity and kindness. He is humble and easy to get along with, and it doesn't surprise me in the least that he would be a natural open channel for spirit to communicate through.

He once did a reading for me when I was going through a difficult period and he brought my grandmother through, describing accurately the exact twinset red knit cardigan and jumper I so fondly remember her wearing and her distinctly shaped glasses.

When his father took ill, he knew he wouldn't have long to say his goodbyes and it was within the week that he deteriorated quite rapidly and was taken to hospital. The family did the familiar roster of someone always being present, and extended family members were contacted to alert them to the news that soon he would be passing. Although he could not ascertain an exact date, they all knew he didn't have that much longer.

Robert spent his days doing his normal tradie job but finishing early to go to the hospital daily just to be there with his father, should it be his time to pass, as he didn't want to miss it.

It was a busy metropolitan Melbourne hospital with the usual goings on – medical emergencies, nurses rushing to and from patients, checking medication charts, liaising with families and buzzers going off with sounds emanating from every corner, every minute and every hour of the day.

On one of these busy afternoons in the corridor of the busy hospital, Robert saw clearly a man walking with an IV pole. That's not so unusual an occurrence in a hospital. The only difference with this man that Robert saw was that 'he wasn't actually alive'; he was in spirit. He stated he got quite a shock seeing him there and he thought to himself, *Oh, what is he doing here, just appearing like that?*

Robert knew enough to know not to be scared and just went with the flow of the vision. Talented as he was sensitive and kind, Robert was picking up on Spirit. The why and wherefore he couldn't answer and he still can't to this day, but he saw him pop out of nowhere. Was it a residual energy of a spirit coming through who had been a patient formerly and Robert was now picking up on? In some strange ethereal way, it was comforting to know that the world of spirit was just a breath away as he waited patiently for his beloved father to cross from our world to the next.

Ben

Ben and I had been friends and he would quite often visit some of the psychic shops that were emerging in Melbourne. He was into learning as much as he could on the topic and was quite a healer. He had a laidback kind of approach to him and he asked me one day if I might do a reading for him. I had been working at a store in St Kilda and doing readings on the weekend. Mindful not to drain myself, I suggested that he come to my mother's place where occasionally I would read. Her place was next to a church and the room that I read in was adjacent to the church and had a beautiful light that emanated from it.

He was very spiritual person himself and open to whatever came through. As I sat with him, I began to see a disturbing vision of a car accident. At times when I see such a thing, it can be difficult and stopping seems easier because of the heartache and terror that the recipient of the reading could feel.

I said to him, 'Ben, I'm sorry but I see a car accident.'

He nodded his head and said, 'Yes, that's right.'

The confirmation was enough to further fuel the reading and so I kept on going. 'I'm now being taken into the bush. It looks beautiful and I can see old gum trees and brush branches along with overgrown grass.'

Again he said, 'Yes, that's right.'

I was feeling that someone was trying to communicate with him and it was almost as if I wasn't me anymore; I was becoming the spirit that was trying to get through.

'I'm given a brother and he is showing me that he is standing next to the car as well.'

Again, he said, 'Yes.'

'It's your brother, isn't it, Ben?'

Again with a saddened and shocked look, he said, 'Yes, my brother passed from a car accident.'

I sensed his brother had more to say and so I closed my eyes to see what else there was and I saw a gorgeous dog, a blue heeler, standing next to the overturned car and his brother.

I said, 'Ben, I have your brother here saying the dog is with him, too. Does that make sense?'

Tears were in his eyes as he replied, 'Yes, when my brother died, the dog was in the car with him and it also passed, they were found together.'

Again the spirit wanted to add more and so as I listened more carefully I heard the name Mark. I said, 'Ben, I'm hearing the name Mark. Does that mean anything to you in regard to your brother?'

'Yes, his name was Marcus.'

'Ben, he is sending his love.'

As I said that the vision of him was so clear, it was as if he were sitting right next to me and that the bush was almost touchable. It appeared as if the veil between this world and the next had been removed so as to reveal to him that all was well. He was letting his brother know that although he was gone from this world he was still able to get a message of love through. The evidence of the car accident and the dog was able to give integrity and proof of survival to Ben.

Another of my readings with Ben was very interesting. As he sat down, I tuned into his work with an Aboriginal singer and that this would be a wonderful opportunity for him. As it turned out, I was right and the musician he was working with was Geoffrey Gurrumul Yunupingu, an Indigenous Australian musician who sang stories of his homeland in his native tongue. Ben worked with him for five years and remembers it as an astonishing piece of information that came through. We were both touched by the reading of his brother and of the message that he was working with an Indigenous artist, who, blind from birth, was one of the most acclaimed Indigenous singers Australia has known.

Walk the walk

I didn't jump into reading professionally. I wanted to take my time. I wanted to test the waters starting with family and friends. It was years before I even thought that perhaps I could work in a shop. The day I summoned up the courage to go and speak to one of the New Age outlets, the first shop owner informed me that she had enough readers. I jumped back into my car thinking, *Oh well, now what?* Then I heard a voice clairaudiently, literally telling me to go to St Kilda as there was a new manager who had taken over a shop. That's what I did as I trusted what was given.

I had an image of the place as well. When I walked in I said, 'I'm just wondering if there is any opportunity for work. I'm a medium and I thought the shop may have been taken over by new management.'

'Yes, it has. I'm the new manager.'

Thank you, Spirit. It was my time to be out there reading.

And so it went from there. I had to do an interview read, but I got the job. I have since worked in shops and I am grateful for the experience. I've read for many, thousands actually, probably around the vicinity of 8,000. I was always passionate about the sacredness of the field and stuck to my own way of reading. Although I had taught myself how to use the tarot cards, my readings were spirit-based. I don't use the cards much at all, because I found they made my reading rigid. So I stuck to the way I was mentored and it served me well.

I came in contact with people who were like me, the birds of the feather. I maintained my individuality. We never stop learning and I tried as best I could to be kind, reverent and to learn and read and absorb what I could. Serving Spirit.

Spirits have a sense of humour

I'm back-tracking to when I had split from a major love in my life. Devastated by the loss of the relationship and living in a share household, I was growing accustomed to a new life. In many ways, I didn't want to rush for the spiritual growth that seems to be everywhere these days. Perhaps many of you reading this book will have done courses and development training in some form or other. Please don't get me wrong, this is fabulous and we all grow in our own ways. What I wish to bring to light here is the natural flow of growth as we develop and train, without being in a hurry. All too often I have seen students and others wanting it too much, and forgetting about the true essence of healing for the other. I believe to grow and to develop without ego or force is a beautiful thing and can set you apart from the crowd.

Retain your individuality because when you start acting as a conduit for the spirit world you can be tested from time to time. Recheck every now and then: where does my integrity lie? What is the higher meaning in situations? Am I acting in line with my ethical and moral code of conduct here? Be grateful – where ribbons of tears flow in the uniting of Spirit from those here still grieving with those on the other side coming through profoundly changes the status quo of preconceived beliefs.

I was single again and, as a bit of a laugh, I said to my flatmates, 'If anyone was to ask, please just tell them that I'm seeing a new guy and his name's Humphrey.'

It was a bit of a laugh and as I swilled back a glass of red, I thought it was funny and kind of therapeutic to imagine myself with a new guy with this name.

It went on for about two weeks or so of finding myself saying, 'Yes, well, you can tell them as well, I'm seeing Humphrey now.'

Later, I got a phone call from a choreographer friend. She said, 'Ronda, I just wanted to see if you were interested in doing a fill-in gig with Humphrey B Bear?'

I was gobsmacked to say the least. 'Um, what?'

She said, 'Humphrey B Bear.'

'OMG, yes, of course, yes.'

I wasn't doing readings professionally at the time but what I'm trying to explain here is the natural way of being in tune. When I got off the phone, my friend who was living with me was at home.

I said, 'OMG, you won't believe this!'

'What? Believe what?'

'Guess who I'm working with next week?'

'Who?'

'Humphrey B Bear!'

There was a roar of thunderous laughter, and I nearly split my sides as well.

I was so nervous learning the script that while going out to buy groceries in a busy centre, I forgot where I had parked my car. I had memorised the script, though.

Trust what you're given. Now later on in life, I look back at this scenario and it makes me smile. To some extent there is always going to be a natural flow with Spirit. I liken it to music and flowing with the beauty of the vibe. That probably sounds a bit OTT. When we are in the process of creating something that is beautiful and we are focused and our integrity and purity of heart and mind are in the moment, it's a beautiful thing and our manner of communicating will be perfect without being perfect.

Thank you, Spirit, for getting me ready, ready for the gig, ready to trust my instincts a little better, and ready to start a new life, even if it was with the little chicken dance that Humphrey is famous for.

Psychic medium and the aura

Our aura is like the reflection of our soul and a psychic can tap into it. The aura can tell us about the past and present and even provide a glimpse of a future possibility; albeit knowing that we all have free will. Our subconscious mind is at work when reading the aura and our clairvoyance, clairaudience and clairsentience (the main three psychic senses) can pick up information. We have clairallience (to smell), clairgustance (to taste) and claircognisance (to know). The first three are our main faculties that are used and most are stronger in one. Some have the three major faculties working all at the same time.

Thoughts can be harmful and may not always have the best intentions, whether deliberate or not. As a psychic, it's possible to tune into thought, tune into the invisible. Being so sensitive our energy can be drained. This could be by a friend, colleague or even family member and although not intentionally sending out harmful thoughts, can affect our energy. I'd like to stress that it may not be intentional but it can have a negative spin on things.

I'd like to take you back to the scene in the book where I could quite visibly see a friend's aura. It was green, a vivid green and quite solid in colour. They were not aware of my being able to see their aura at the time but it was a clear indication of vibes being sent out. This was a clear look at what can be directed. Again we are energy, not just the physical. How many times have you heard someone say something but known that what they actually meant was the opposite of what was being said?

Stand back, you've just absorbed the energy and not the words. This happens to all of us.

This interaction can drain us. I'd like to give you an example.

Amber had an unhappy marriage and had resorted to drinking on a regular basis. Her friends at the time came to see her with their respective partners. In part due to her own unhappiness, she created discord and arguments in her friends' relationships, gossiping about various details she knew would upset each partner and causing pain and grief. Upon leaving the premises, anger would be etched onto their faces when they had previously arrived all bubbly and happy.

She was consciously and unconsciously attacking the energy fields of others negatively and it caused harm and created a ripple effect that exists to this very day. Friends left and didn't return, and relationships were harmed. It is not uncommon to leave such an interaction drained of energy and tired. A symptom. The energy can also be infused with jealousy, envy, competitiveness, all of the negative elements that might in any type of energy interaction be exhausting.

A sensitive or psychic is very exposed to this type of exchange due to their sensitivity. We can all at times do this; we ourselves can be the negativity without even being aware.

The aura is not only affected by soul energy. Drugs and alcohol. Our good intentions, our bad thoughts. Our grace, kindness. Jealousy was what I saw, the vivid green aura around a friend. The psychic faculties will work with sensing the colour and density of the auras and, as you develop, so does your clairvoyancy in response to auric fields and their meanings. Clairvoyance here means seeing and interpreting the aura. As well as clairvoyantly seeing the auric field, you may sense the feeling without seeing any colour. You may be clairsentiently picking up on a mood like happiness or sadness within the field. In other words, your gut may be telling you.

The aura is constantly changing in colour, form and density. You might notice that subconsciously when people feel threatened or you yourself feel defensive, you will fold your arms over each other and even sway back a little. Being aware that we are more than the physical and that we are energy can help to comprehend the essence of being a spirit here too in the body on the physical plane. In that way it may be easier to understand the idea of the light body around us and how it can be affected emotionally. The down side of being sensitive is that we can be 'overly sensitive' to some situations but the up side of it is that we can readily tune in to situations and then read them picking up on things that perhaps others may not have seen because of this faculty.

I've witnessed colours and auras in differing situations connected to health, emotions and love. I believe Spirit works with me to tune me in and that is why I receive aura-based information at times.

Your energy field is opened up to the spirit world if you are a medium by nature. When reading, it's also opened up to the energy of the person receiving the reading. I always say a little prayer and thank Spirit for working through me and I try to open myself in as pure a light as possible with a pure intention. I connect through my own aura and the consciousness that my heart centre is open. I've let love fuel my mediumship. Many simply tune in without any ritualistic opening or closing of energy centres. When I sat in circle and trained, we were taught to open and close the energy centres.

During a platform demonstration, I will often see a flash of light or shade with people in the congregation and know that someone in the spirit world is wishing to make contact with that person. Sometimes I will see images of faces or animals standing next to a person. These images are hazy but there are cases where mediums have seen the other side very clearly indeed.

I have come to value the aura and pay more attention to the energy of myself and others. Keeping my energy, my heart clear is important, because it is a mirror of the emotions, mind, body and spirit of us all. Nice to know that we not only have a physical body but also have an energetic body. This light body around us can pick up on feelings and sensations to alert us. With this in mind, we can be more mindful of the substances that we put into our body and the thoughts we carry in our minds and hearts.

If we are drained of energy and feeling lethargic the aura itself, too, can dull, as opposed to if we are full of life, charged with positive energy – then our aura is more vibrant in colour. Thinking dark, depressed thoughts can also dull the aura, as can an illness or lovesick heart. Going for a walk in a garden or being around animals can fill the spirit and the auric field with love.

As sensitive beings ourselves, we can be affected by another person's energy field. The danger of not recognising this type of energy is that it can hang around and block the flow of good energy. This means you can take the bad energy home and it could make you feel grumpy and polluted somehow – it can also effect the flow of energy between yourself and your loved ones. Because a psychic's energy field is sensitive, it is not uncommon to pick up this vibration. It might be a downside of the gift of psychic awareness but being aware that this could happen, being in tune with energies and being responsible enough to clear away any toxic deposits can facilitate the best flow possible.

We don't have to become infiltrated with another person's energy. We can be responsible for the health and nurturing of our own good energy. In this way we can best serve Spirit and be the best conduit.

If we liken the idea of mediumship to a radio station and the idea of the best possible frequency being able to reach the spirit world effectively without any interruptions or static, then you may have a better idea of how energy and the auric field can help to facilitate the transmission of messages from the spirit world. We raise our vibration to work with the spirit world. As mediums, we have built power through our own spiritual practices and through faith and experience.

Animals

When I first started reading, I never thought about animals and the way they cross over just as we do. We had a cat, part ragdoll and part tabby, we bought from a breeder – my daughter lovingly named him Pickles. He passed not long after we got him, only a few months old. We were devastated.

I remember going to see my mentor Jill and she said, 'I'm being told that you have lost an animal.'

You could have knocked me over with a feather. I love all animals and, like most of us, knowing they also pass over and will come through in readings gives me great comfort. I have done readings since the day Jill taught me this inadvertently and have seen animals in spirit reunite with their owners. It's a beautiful energy and humbling to witness. I will see them as they were in colour and size, although I don't know the breeds well enough to say what they are. I'm learning this is a reference point to be able to give to the owners. It's nice to know they want to be remembered, and cherish the time they were with you. I usually see them with a paw up on the leg of the owner or they'll wander into the reading when you least expect them. Happy and full of joy and love. They will put their head on your leg and rest there. They will come through and place themselves in a way that is specific to the way you cared for them.

While nursing I got to know Elsie, one of my regular patients. She had suffered tremendously in this life. I recall one morning we were chatting about animals and she told me that she had lost a beloved pet, a little terrior name Beau. She stated that one morning while she was at home only weeks or so after her pet passed, she was in the shower and could distinctly hear the sound of a dog barking. She knew that the barking was from her dog in spirit. This was something that Beau would usually do. She stated it wasn't the first time she had heard the dog bark after it had passed.

One very dear medium friend held a class weekly for his students where he would teach them to connect psychically and assist them in opening up to Spirit in order to help them develop their skills in mediumship. As a special class he thought it would be a good idea to take his students to a nearby mini farm to see what they could psychically glean from the animals.

One of his students had come across a few horses in a paddock. The student walked over to the fence and a horse came across. As the horse came closer, the student felt that the horse was sad and he picked up that she wasn't performing as well as the other horses. He thought it was a bit strange but he relayed this message on to the teacher.

Later in the day the owner of the property came over and spoke to my friend – he relayed the message that the student had given him, that one of her horses felt she wasn't performing as well as the other horses. The owner of the property laughed as she told my friend the other horses in the paddock had all received ribbons for awards but she hadn't.

I have to say this is a part of the work that I really love. It's usually very moving and is a reminder that we are all connected to those we have loved, even our cherished pets that break through the ether into a reading of a dearly beloved owner to let them know how they appreciated the care and love they received while on this plane of existence.

Fine-tuning

Signs and symbols will help to assist in a reading and help decipher and decode information that comes through from the spirit world. As you will recall from the earlier chapters, I was given a black cross when dealing with death. Signs and symbols can also change from time to time as you develop and become more adept.

It's also important to remember that each person we read for has a unique energy and so we receive unique information, and it's imperative to read the symbols that you see according to the energy that you are picking up on for that particular person. All too often I have seen psychics giving readings and referring to symbols that they use and giving out the same generic information for each reading or client.

I saw a lily appear over my mother as we sat having a cup of tea and I said to her that I thought Aunty Esmeralda may cross soon. She, in fact, passed the next day. Now you could say, why didn't I see the black cross like I had before? I thought that too, yet I knew as soon as I had (clairvoyantly) seen the lily that it was a sign and it belonged to my aunty Esmeralda.

So I was clairvoyantly seeing the sign and clairsentiently (instinctively) knew it belonged to my aunty. The signs will come but, more importantly, you need to be aware of them. Take note and quietly let them sink in. You can always reflect on it later. Read it as it is given and if it makes sense at the time, take notice. All the senses will be involved in giving signs or the senses that are strongest for you. It may be more of a gut feeling – clairsentience. It could be that you feel something isn't right with a certain person – they may be smiling and working as if nothing has changed but your feeling deep down is that something just isn't right. Spirit will show me a birthday cake for a birthday or a gift of flowers. I will also get red roses as a sign of romance in the air but I may also be given something different in regards to romance such as a love heart; it just depends.

A lot of psychics will pre-program their own set of signs and symbols and that's okay too, but keep in mind we evolve. For a medium who works with Spirit, they use what is in the mind of the medium as references and what knowledge they have learned and experienced as a reference point. So the more reference points the better.

Your guides will work with you and give signs and differing symbols and these will be developed and built up over time as your references develop. Sometimes the signs will be really strong and hard to dismiss and at other times they will be subtle. I remember the very first sign that Spirit gave me in connection to someone's health. It was a red china teapot, mentioned earlier, quite colourful with a sense that a herbal tea was brewing in it. I knew what the message was as I delivered it.

'You need to be more mindful of your health and diet, and what you are putting into your body. I'm being shown a teapot with herbal tea.'

Sometimes the sign will be as you see it and you won't need to decipher it. At other times, you will need to decode it. The sign was interpreted clairvoyantly so I could see in my mind's eye, the third eye.

It's also a good idea to keep a journal and look back on it from time to time as you see your work evolve and your signs and symbols grow. Journalling is a great reflection companion to assess your development. Reference points will emerge as the journey of life continues and new experiences come.

Journals also help us to see what serves us and where we could grow mediumistically or psychically by honestly writing about our development and our understanding. We may also tune into deeper thoughts about our readings and work through journaling.

Psychic senses

To give information to the sitter – that is, the person coming for a reading or in a platform demonstration – I need to be able to decipher what's coming through so that it can be passed on accordingly. Like a frequency and an instrument that is finely tuned, the psychic senses help decode the messages both psychically and mediumistically. Quite often one ability may be stronger to begin with or it may be that we tend to focus more intently on one as we begin.

Clairvoyance

Clairvoyance, which is the French word for clear seeing, is to see information visually through the third eye. Information that is psychic and mediumistic. The sight is through mental images in the mind's eye or to even see beyond what is presented to us, that being the truth of the matter.

I also may see something ahead of our time as, when I'm reading, it can feel as if I'm almost outside of time. So I'm picking up on Grandpa Joe or Aunty Belle but they have passed over so they are not living in 'the now'. This also includes seeing things from the past – that is, retrocognition, which means backwards knowing. Remote viewing is another aspect of clairvoyancy – that is, seeing things without actually having ever viewed the target or seeing things from a distance. Like describing the exact colour of the cushions that are in a house you have never visited.

Objective clairvoyance is seeing spirit appear as in an apparition. This occurrence is extremely rare but it has happened and it takes more energy for the spirit on the other side to come through. They can appear in a form that is dense and very human-like or in a hazier form where we recognise them but they appear 'see through'.

Tuning in and becoming more aware of scenery, paintings, designs and things of a visual nature assist in developing this ability, but it doesn't mean that you need to be artistic. It's just that this ability is stimulated by such things and taking notice.

Clairaudience

Clairaudience, from the French word meaning clear hearing, is to receive messages through the sense of inner hearing. I will hear messages from those passed over to bring to those on this side. Sometimes it may be a name, or it may be information pertaining to the sitter that I could not possibly have known. It's like hearing in the physical world we live in but it resonates in a different area of my mind so I'm hearing information internally, within my mind. Spirit communicates telepathically.

Sometimes it can be external – this is rarer though, and is called objective clairaudience. It is witnessed sometimes in psychic circles or in trance demonstrations where groups have heard spirit voices. Earlier in the book I mentioned hearing my father's voice after he had passed away, giving me a warning about a guy I was seeing. His voice was clear and when I first developed clairaudience I had to discern whether or not I was hearing my own thoughts as opposed to Spirit. Again, it's a different vibration and as you become used to hearing clairaudiently, it becomes easier to discern between the two.

Psychically we can tune into information for a sitter using clairaudience, where we hear information coming into our mind as opposed to seeing or feeling the information. This ability may come naturally with clairvoyance or may develop after other abilities are formed. Tuning into sounds can stimulate and develop this ability.

Clairsentience

To feel. Have you ever had one of those moments when you felt something just doesn't feel right? The feeling is in the pit of your stomach, what others may call a gut feeling. Furthermore, it turned out to be right. Spirit will quite often relay the feeling of an experience, the feeling of the love they had for a person. Spirit will again be communicating telepathically because that is how they communicate. Spirit may communicate to me something like Aunty Alice was always nervous in the car and she didn't drive. The sitter will then be able to confirm that yes, Aunty Alice was like that. I will glean that information from feeling nervous about the car as I'm delivering the information.

Spirit may also show me something but deliver it in a way that I will feel it first. I may receive a pain in my leg and then say to the sitter Spirit is showing me that you have recently had trauma to the leg. Spirit is relaying the message clairsentiently. I had a family who had come for a reading and I felt that I had a sore back while tuning into the grandmother. As it turned out, the grandmother had had back surgery around eight months prior to the reading. I had tuned into her husband in spirit who was giving me that message clairsentiently. He also went on to say he was sorry that she had been in so much pain because he loved her so much.

Psychically, it may be that we feel someone else's pain and in that way we are picking up on that energy clairsentiently. Clairsentience is linked in with empathy. This ability is stimulated by being sensitive and having empathy whereby we can access feelings more readily as opposed to shutting down that faculty.

Clairallience

The sense of smell can be relayed by Spirit. Spirit will use the sense of smell as a reference point in order to get the message across. It may be that the scent of a favourite cologne or perfume comes through. I have heard a couple of people state after a relative passed they could smell their perfume. Once when I was sitting in a psychic circle, the six of us could all smell lemons in the room during one session. Quite amazing but a good example of clairallience. This was even objective clairallience as instead of the smell being transmitted through the mind of the medium only, all six of us could distinctly smell lemons. I never doubted that ability again.

My mentor always told us that when she passed we would smell cigarettes because she smoked. She had cancer of the colon and the night she passed, I dreamt that I was an Indian girl. I knew I was because in my dream I was looking in the mirror and the texture of my skin was different. I woke up, not really putting it all together, really just thinking how strange that I should dream that. In the back of my mind I was wondering how Jill was as I knew she was going downhill. She had an Indian guide, Vashti, that's why I was thinking of her as I dreamt of being Indian, although I didn't think of that at the time.

That morning at work, the call came through. One of her daughters rang to say she had passed away in the early hours of the morning. When the daughters arrived at the house, hours after her passing, they informed those of us who were close to her that they could smell cigarette smoke in the room quite distinctly. With family by her side as she lay in the bed, she had not been smoking and there was previously no hint of cigarette odours. Spirits do their best to give us the signs from the other side.

Clairgustance

Clairgustance is the ability to taste without anything being in the mouth. For example, to sense a substance that perhaps someone in the realm of the spirit world liked to eat or drink like chocolate cake or wine. The sensation of actually being able to taste it momentarily is there. For example, it could have been that the person had a cake shop and suddenly you can taste cakes. I remember reading for a friend once and saying to her that I felt dizzy and intoxicated. She fessed up and told me she had just had a glass of wine. As I was tuning in to her, I felt tipsy. Although it wasn't spirit giving me information, I was psychically picking up on her status.

Claircognisance

Claircognisance is an ability to know something without any prior knowledge or information provided. It simply comes through as a certain knowledge that the soul affirms. It can almost seem like an 'A-ha!' moment, and the certainty sits comfortably with us. For example, we know the person we have just met is no good, or we know that there is something wrong with a house we've just entered. It's like all of the clair abilities are switched on at once and the feeling just comes straight through to us. We may just know that a job will land on our desk within days. It's difficult to pinpoint exactly how we know but the resounding thoughts are that it is a cosmic universal energy that we can tap into.

The connection

The spirit world do the very best they can when coming through in platform demonstrations and readings alike. It never ceases to amaze me. How lucky and blessed we really are.

These senses are used for us like a radar to download information and each one may be used independently or combined, depending on what has been developed.

Physical mediumship can involve smells, levitation, drafts, apportation of objects, spirit lights, knocking or rapping sounds, and even direct voice communication. More than one person can witness physical mediumship to attest to its wonder.

You may recall earlier in the book my account of the beer can moving and you may recall my story of hearing my father's voice after he passed. Here is another example of the wonder of the spirit realm.

I was driving to my mother's house while she was living with my sister. It was a sunny day and visibility was good. As I drove into her street I noticed her headlights flashing. They flashed a couple of times. I thought it odd, but that she must be going out and had accidently flashed the headlights on so I pulled up alongside of her car. She wasn't actually in the car. My mother is in her eighties. I went to the front door as I thought she might be playing with the remote from inside the house.

I asked her when she opened the door, 'Were you trying to open the car door from inside the house?'

She said, 'No, as if that would work.'

I laughed and asked my nephew who was at home whether he was trying or saw her with the keys. He replied no and queried why.

This one is still unanswered, folks, but I felt that Dad wasn't happy about her driving. This type of occurrence is a good example of physical mediumship, manipulating an object that has electrical activity.

Meditation

Stilling the mind is good for a focus to declutter the information that the mind can collect. Like, I must drop off that jacket to the dry cleaners, and I must not forget to pick up the computer part for the PC – all of that. The example I like the best and one that I learned through teachers is the image of a still lake. It is a good idea to meditate at least twice a week. In the Buddhist faith, meditation is revered as an important aspect on the path to enlightenment and nirvana. Meditation is believed to increase healing and creative abilities. Mantras or the repetition of holy words can be used to achieve an enhanced calm and meditative state within. The mind is used to connect with the spirit world and to blend with the mind of the spirit discarnate and, as that connection is sacred, so too then is the mind that is used to assist. Treating the mind with respect is akin to the wisdom of the soul. Meditation can be used to relax or for more focused work like connecting to the Creator. There are also guided meditations that can assist with things like meeting spirit guides. Meditation can quieten the mind.

A lot of times prior to a psychic or mediumship reading or platform demonstration, psychics and mediums have been known to meditate. However, this is not recommended by some as meditation quietens the mind down and we need to be energised and fully vibrant to connect in with the spirit world and with our minds to fully receive messages. If we are in a passive state of mind, we could miss out on certain messages.

A stitch in time

I had worked with a singer named Julie Cook. Her voice was totally awesome and she was an understudy in the musical *Jesus Christ Superstar*. She had a soulful voice and an immense range. We became friends after singing in a band. We just clicked as she had a great sense of humour and we had a camaraderie that musicians have. She became unwell suddenly and moved interstate to be with family. We kept in contact over the phone, and she was in and out of hospital regularly. Julie was so down to earth; she never had the materialistic things that some people have but she had a heart of gold and the voice of an angel.

I was well into nursing on a ward at a busy metropolitan hospital when she became gravely ill. As I was driving home from a late shift, I heard 'Julie'. I thought to myself, *Oh, I must ring*. The next day the same thing happened during the day as I pulled up to get petrol. 'Julie, ring.' *Mmm*, I thought, *gosh I must ring Julie*. The following day after another late shift, 'Julie'.

So when I got home, I rang and her sister answered. 'Ron, where have you been? We have been trying to call you, Julie is about to pass.'

My heart stopped a beat. My beautiful dear friend who had taught me so much about music and humility was about to die. She was on her death bed in the hospital. I had changed my phone number and they couldn't get through. I could have rung earlier just to hear her voice that one last time and to let her know that I will always be grateful for the friendship, will always adore her and will miss her. And when it's my time I will look for her and we will sing up a storm on the other side.

She passed peacefully into the arms of the angels and she left my daughter and I money, enough to have a holiday and buy my daughter a computer. We just cried. As I was telling my daughter she had left us money, tears were falling down and my daughter was crying, too.

The message here, as you may have twigged, is listen to that inner voice. It's there for all of us to hear and to tune into. We get lost sometimes in what appears to be really important. For me, saying goodbye was really important. I know in my heart and soul she would have loved to have heard my voice telling her it's okay, don't be afraid and I didn't get the chance to do that. I could have if I had listened, if I had trusted the urgency. Here I was the medium and doing readings and I didn't listen. I wanted to say goodbye. I just wanted to be there and say goodbye, I will see you again, and I will hear you sing …

Trust

When I first started doing readings, with some of the experiences I had I wondered at times if I were going a bit mad. Then I got confirmation through evidence from the people that I was reading for and it made it all worthwhile. Being able to connect people here with loved ones who had crossed over was worth it. It was worth every experience I had to go through. I got to know some other psychics through working in the field and we would at times swap readings. Louise Bolger, a renowned psychic medium in her own right and friend, had invited me over to her place for such a swap, and her reading was wonderful and she was able to pinpoint details, including my grandfather's name, with accuracy. When I started up her reading, I looked over at the doorway and could see the image of a nurse all dressed in white with a red cross.

I said, 'Louise, your grandmother is showing me a nurse's outfit with a red cross.'

She explained that her grandmother was one of the first nurses to work for the Red Cross in Australia. My message here is to trust what you are given. Don't second-guess it, just go with it. Spirits try their best to come through with the most ardent images and messages they can to get through to their loved ones. I had to trust the information that I was receiving clairvoyantly. I'm glad I did; it gave a sense of sacredness to the energy we were part of.

I'm also a big believer in being humble and gracious and thanking Spirit, being part of a team and being a good team player.

Absent healing

When I first started out, we would do absent healing as part of our regime in the mentoring group. We would send energy through colours out to those who were suffering. This technique is still used in spiritual circles and churches today. This helped in working with the aura and in the area of receiving colours from guides and using differing shades to assist in the healing of those who were unwell. You don't have to be artistic with the work of colour in the aura – more importantly, it is the intention that you have towards those you wish to heal. Intention is key. It's not about the money or the cloak you wear. Being a medium is about the connection and the effect it has both for those receiving the message here on this side and the spirit world who have done their best to come through and deliver.

Guides

I am part of a team and like other mediums out there, I have guides that assist in working with me as a vessel, as the conduit for the message of those in Spirit. It is said that guides are spirits that may have walked the earth before in another time, or we may have had a connection to them in another lifetime. Like a guardian angel, we have a master guide.

I connected with my guide for the first time through a psychic circle. It took a couple of sessions to feel comfortable and I remember feeling a buzz in my head quite distinctly and heard a name, Yukky.

I was embarrassed and said, 'Yes, I am getting a name and it's Yukky.'

Well, upon trying again, I discovered the name is Yuki, a Japanese name. She has a serene and beautiful presence when I connect to her.

It isn't important or essential to always get a name when your guides comes through. More than anything, you will sense a feeling and essence of Spirit and a familiarity of that presence as you begin to learn to trust and work with them. They also have to learn to work with us as well so dedicating time to allocate sensing their energetic qualities is a good idea. Again, remain humble and have only the best intentions and respect when working with your guides – remember it's an honour.

Knowing that they wish to work with us and assist is a powerful thing. Remaining open-minded is a good start and trying not to force any type of connection is warranted as it takes time and focus. Main guides can also change depending on our development, our needs and the role that they play.

While doing readings in shops I noticed a flash of a vision of a nun in spirit one day. I was surprised at first but I recognised that this image would present itself at times. Guides can change as the work you do changes and evolves. Some attest to family members in the spirit world as their guides. Guides will be attracted to certain energies and qualities of the medium as they blend with us while we work. I'm ever grateful to be working for Spirit and not a day goes by that I don't appreciate the care and loving energies that I work with.

I liken working with guides, like an interpreter that might speak another language. The theory when I first began is that the guide was in the middle of spirit communication and would receive messages from the soul in spirit and relay it to the medium, and then the medium would relay the message to the recipient.

These days there is a much simpler explanation, and it is that as a medium we connect directly to the soul in spirit and can bring through messages to the recipient. The guides know how we best work and they are aware of our specific skill set. Sometimes guides will change depending on our specific level of development and need. I know that my guide has worked with me for a long time. I have a strong relationship with her on the other side and I'm continually grateful for her compassion and understanding. I believe that she too, is very creative and imaginative and works with me on that level.

I have read for people who have had grandparents or parents from other countries so that they are not English-speaking and the messages are still able to be translated in spirit, through the essence of what the soul in spirit is trying to convey. During one reading, I said the word 'wait' in Slovakian, which came through from the grandmother. It made sense to the sitter at the time. I had no idea what it meant. She had been in a relationship that was going really badly.

The grandmother kept saying the word in Czech and her granddaughter said, 'I know what she means, she is saying wait for the right man to come along.'

The beauty of recognising the guide is that it can increase a student's confidence when they are a beginner. Quite often I have found that students are comfortable knowing that someone in spirit is dedicated to working with them and that they are not alone in the process of spirit communication.

Back in the day, our original circles consisted of between six and eight members. We would link in with a spirit through our guides, and it was also customary then to open and close the chakras before commencing work with spirit. It was a rarer thing to stumble upon a circle in those days and was usually facilitated by a member of one of the spiritualist churches.

I was lucky to have had the mentorship.

Nonetheless the circle was run in a disciplined way and we sat for nine months. It is incredible to sit in a psychic circle that is run by an established medium as you can feel a shift in the energy in the room and in yourself as you partake in the phenomena of communicating with spirit. These days, one is more likely to find a development group or attend workshops in the area of their particular interest. I have run several groups, some from home and others from places where I have taught.

The power

People will speak of 'sitting in the power', and building the power to blend with the spirit world. Spirit is there for us to connect to infinitely – it's a matter of us being ready and open to the connection. Having respect for that power and treating it as sacred is paramount as the world opens up to this new wave of consciousness. We all have within us that spark of divinity, we all are light. As Spirit gets to know our unique gifts, Spirit can work with them. Because I worked musically and have a trained ear, I have found that I can be quite clairaudient and good with names and chatting to spirits. Also because I'm artistic and visual, they can imprint images onto my mind and I can decipher those in a unique way to inform the sitter or audience if I'm working platform. Sitting in the power takes discipline and focus but it is worth the effort as Spirit gets to know us and our skill set more deeply. It is different from meditation, because it is sitting for the spirit world and does take discipline as our busy cluttered minds can intervene.

Sitting for the spirit world also helps us to connect in to our own divinity and the sense of us being a spirit in a physical body. This can help our mediumship to develop more as we recognise that we are spirit and as we attune to the world of spirit it can assist with the blending of spirit in this world to that of the other. It can help us to build our power when working and sustain links from the spirit world when reading for others and in platform demonstrations.

As we begin to know ourselves as a spiritual being, we can open to the spirit world as a spiritual being to blend with them and receive messages. It can also help to differentiate a differing energy as opposed to our own spirit. Aligning to that attunement can assist in reading as a psychic and as a medium. Knowing as a spirit we are a force, and opening to God/Creator and that power of spirit that we all are is important. Sensing spirit and sensing the divine, feeling the force work through us as part of us and how, as force, the vibration of thoughts affect us. Feeling the interconnectedness of the universe we are a part of. To know the other, we need to know ourselves. To blend and work with Spirit, we need to access our own spirit and its wonder here on the earthly plane.

When we work with spirits, we raise our vibration to connect with them, and sitting in the power can assist with that. Some may walk near the ocean, play music, dance, laugh or be in nature. Raising my vibration invigorates my energy as opposed to being down and negative and full of fear. Raising my vibration tells me that love is king to connect with those in the other world.

The third eye

When we open our eyes to the light, we open to the light of the soul.

The third eye is thought to provide insight beyond ordinary vision. A kind of extra awareness of what is taking place. It has been noted symbolically as thus. It is connected to the idea of higher consciousness and related to clairvoyance, hence the idea of 'seers'. It can also be associated with states of enlightenment. Situated between the two physical eyes and extending up to the forehead as it is thought when fully opened. The third eye has also rods and cones; the human pineal gland which some refer to as the third eye contains retinal tissue within; like the physical eye.

The pineal gland is in the centre of the brain and it corresponds to the sixth chakra, of the third eye. The main cells of the pineal gland are pinealocytes. The main function of the pinealocytes is the secretion of melatonin, which regulates circadian rhythms, and so influences sleep cycles and sexual development in the brain and body.

It has been described as the 'seat of the soul', the spiritual antenna, giving inner vision. The approximate size is that of a raisin.

Research today explores the religious philosophies of the past and the connection to the drug DMT and its hallucinogenic properties enabling other world communications and higher levels of consciousness.

In ancient Egypt the pineal gland was symbolised through the eye of Horus, and the symbolism of the eye has been passed down throughout the ages.

At the top of the Budda's head a pine cone shape is seen and at the area of the pineal gland/third eye there is sometimes a dot on the forehead, a symbol of the third eye and knowledge within, esoteric awakening.

If we take for example observing a medium whilst on platform delivering messages out to a crowd the third eye area is working hard receiving images of perhaps what a person looked like before they crossed over, what the house they lived in was like, the car they would drive and even the type of cat they may have had. They are receiving images in their minds eye. This 'seeing' ability otherwise known as clairvoyance is vital in playing a role in being able to work both on a psychic and mediumistic level. Some attest to the idea of meditation to stimulate the awakening of this area.

People will often ask a psychic and medium 'what are you seeing'. It's not just the third eye at work and in time we may unravel the link even further. I remember when I was first developing in training I would get a buzz in my forehead when connecting in and reading for another. It doesn't happen now but I've often thought about the third eye area as I'm aware that it is very 'awake' during readings. Being mindful of that I'm also aware that it needs to rest so it's interesting that this area also regulates sleep cycles.

Is it the spiritual gateway to another dimension? Perhaps humans will always be looking for answers to the mystical to quantify and explain that which is outside the rational mind. To paraphrase; Tony Stockwell a noted Psychic Medium in the UK who teaches and demonstrates informs us when interviewed on 'Spirits Voice' on you tube re connecting with spirit; as mediums we are 'merging our soul with the soul of those in spirit to bring forth information aware that the communication is spirit to spirit'. I'm aware of the balancing act that mind body and spirit play to work together and in this way value the third eye area as part of the conduit that mediums are.

Contact

Henry arrived at the hospital as a patient from a nursing home, where he had been living until he caused some disruption. He was moving away from Francine, his girlfriend in the nursing home. In his early days, he was a bit of a genius and had developed a chain of products that was produced in a factory and sold.

He had suffered a brain tumour and, after that, he pretty much lost everything. So as the story goes, he arrived in hospital and I looked after him. Of course, we shouldn't have favourite patients but … He arrived with a bag of clothes and a box of personal items and another cardboard box full of photos of himself and his beloved Francine. I was touched by his humility and, as we rummaged through the photos, I witnessed the life of a man who was much loved and who had contributed to the world in the best way he knew. It was an honour to look after him and I think he could sense that I was genuine and sincere with the care.

He had to be closely supervised as he was an absconding risk, although slow on his feet with his trusty walker. One never knew where one might find him if he wasn't being closely observed. He was a joy to look after, and with the right medications he was calm and settled. I carefully attended to combing his hair and making sure that his socks were on, his jumpsuit was at the right level and he was warm enough. We looked at the photos and, although slow in mind and he struggled at times, he seemed to understand. I sensed he knew I cared and that was enough for him. I couldn't help but feel for Henry – what a life journey and how hard to be pipped at the post with the illness that he suffered and the loss occurring from that. Francine visited him one day and it was evident how happy he was as his ice-blue eyes shone when he glimpsed her walk into the room.

Every time I went to leave the shift, he would walk me to the door to say goodbye on his walker.

He was moved to a different nursing home and Francine passed not long after that. I had been thinking of him – it must have been about four weeks later. I was on holidays and not working at the time but I was wondering how Henry was. This thought became recurring, a nagging that kept going. I returned to work a few days later and, as I walked in, I enquired how he was doing. We had a colleague who worked at the nursing home.

'He's gone; he passed a few weeks after Francine.'

I was happy for him really – he was finally free to be together with his beloved Francine. His journey here had been a tough one, he had suffered, and now his soul could dance with her.

Months later I dreamt a man had come to visit me in my dreams and kissed me on the cheek. I awoke and knew in my heart it was Henry. What he wasn't able to verbalise because of the deficit the brain tumour had left, he was now able to verbalise in a dream. It was a feeling of gratitude. A kiss from the other side.

The gratitude was repaid from 'across the veil' on the other side. The universe is unable to tell me if I was right, because I was physically unable to check on that; yet the timing and the presence felt like Henry was indeed thanking me, letting me know. It was his humility that had caught my attention in the first instance and that same quality shone through even after his passing.

I was so touched, so happy for him – he made it and he was letting me know, thank you. I am eternally grateful.

Watching over us

I had just started doing platform demonstrations and, as students in the field will know, a good way of honing and beginning to do platform is under the guidance of an experienced medium who knows the ropes. I had been in a development circle in my twenties and had done thousands of readings in shops but hadn't done much platform work and I was fearful of speaking in public. I somehow had to get over that fear. I began to do platform at fairs where the general public would be listening and watching fervently. The more experienced medium had handed the baton over to me to perform. I surrendered to Spirit and had been praying the night before for guidance and help. I remember looking out into the audience that had gathered and seeing a shadow behind a girl sitting quietly in one of the back rows.

I said to her, 'Hello, yes, may I come to you?'

'Yes,' she replied.

I said, 'I'm sensing a mother figure in spirit, would I be right saying that?'

'Yes.'

I asked, 'I am being shown that she passed over from a heart attack, is this also correct?'

The woman replied, 'Yes, that is correct.'

'She tells me that you have been through a hard time lately,' I told her.

Again, the woman replied, 'Yes, that's right.'

'I see, and she is telling me that you have lost something.'

'Yes, that's right,' she said.

I then told her, 'She is telling me that she knows of this and is with you. She's telling me that she is aware of your sadness.'

'Yes, that's true.'

I said, 'She's telling me that you have lost something again. I feel that in the lower part of my body, I feel that it's slipped away.'

The woman was crying now. 'Yes.'

I had one last message for her. 'She wants me to let you know how much she loves you and that it will be okay. Everything will be fine, look to a brighter day and she is with you always.'

The woman said, 'Thank you, and I know what she means.'

I had the sense to stop there; she had got this message across and although I wasn't sure what the loss had meant, the message was delivered. After the demonstration was finished the lady in the audience came over to me.

She said, 'I wanted to thank you.'

'Oh, you're absolutely welcome,' I replied.

She told me, 'I believe that was my mother in the spirit world and she has seen that three months ago I had a miscarriage. It was the first time I had tried to conceive.'

'Oh, I'm so sorry to hear that.'

'I'm so glad that she came through to me. I have been so upset but we are trying again,' she said.

'I'm so glad that she came through for you,' I said.

Looking out into the audience, her presence felt so strong and it was the first image that I saw. My gaze just went straight over to her in the small crowd. She wanted if possible to make sure that her daughter knew she was in spirit watching over her. That even though she had passed from this world into the next, she was still the loving parent that she had always been, aware of her despair and longing for a baby and the grief that she was now harbouring. Although in tears as she came over to me, the two of us were in awe at the wonderful way spirits work. It never ceases to amaze me. Receiving and communicating the message with the knowledge that her mother who had indeed passed had helped her in her own way to heal. She was able to look deeper within and know that she too could communicate with her mother in the spirit world. Love never dies.

Nurse Roni

The night before my injury I actually heard a voice say before my shift, 'Don't go.' I thought it was odd and I heard it again, 'Don't go.'

It was tempting to call in and say, 'I'm sorry but I can't come in.' But I said to the voice, which I knew was Spirit, 'I have to go because I can't let the team down.' Again, I heard the voice saying, 'Don't go.'

I was so proud to say that I was a nurse. For me, coming from an artistic background as a singer, it was a huge achievement and I had proved to myself that I could indeed think logically. I could even achieve a 100 per cent pass rate for my maths, which for me was astounding. I was so grateful to be working in such a career and poured my heart out to the patients, giving all I had to be the best caring nurse that I could be.

I remember once getting into a taxi with my sisters as we were going into town – they were chatting in the back seat as I sat in the front. On and on they went, talking about this and that going on in their lives when the driver, a lovely young Indian boy, chirped in.

He said, 'Excuse me but are you still working at the hospital?'

I turned to look at him with my eyes wide open and said, 'Yes, but how do you know I work there?'

My sisters, who were deep in conversation, stopped talking to listen with surprise.

'Oh, I remember you, and you were really nice when one of my friends was waiting for an operation.'

Well, you could have knocked me over with a feather, I felt so humbled and honoured to have been noticed for the care I had given.

And so it went on day after day, shift after shift and medication after medication. At times I had forgotten that I used to sing other than singing along to the tunes in the car. My focus was well and truly on nursing and attending to the daily needs of patients and their families who were at the hospital. I loved every moment of it, even though some of those moments were stressful. I met dedicated and exceptional colleagues with whom I'm friendly to this day. They changed my life – we were the A-team. The doctors, nurses, allied health professionals and porters were some of the most dedicated and hard-working people you could ever wish to meet.

The night of the injury was hard core. We had eight patients, including one lady who was finding it difficult to walk due to a foot injury so she had to be assisted out of her bed to the toilet. She was up again sometimes within a 15-minute interval – I must have assisted her at least 20 to 30 times, probably more. We also had an elderly gentleman with emphysema who needed attention as well as another with military TB. I felt a strain in my right shoulder during the shift.

I was flat out and exhausted by the time it was morning and I had to hand over my patients to the oncoming nurse. When I got home, I collapsed into bed. The next night I did a shift as well, noticing that my arm had been weaker since the afternoon.

As soon as I could, I went to my local GP who thought I had strained my arm. But as the weeks went by, it got worse and worse. Something wasn't right and it became harder to move. As it turned out, I had a tear in my shoulder and was operated on approximately eight months later. What a journey …

Anyone who has gone through WorkCover will likely tell you it's not an easy ride. It's gruelling but I found out who my friends were and are to this day. I was devastated when I was told I couldn't nurse acute patients any more, yet I knew it was for the best. My body wasn't able to sustain the type of nursing that I was previously doing. It was one door closing and another opening up.

I had started on that ward as a clerk and then returned to the ward as a nurse. I was safe and secure, and I thought that I would retire there. No, that was not to be. Life was changing and going in another direction and the struggle and pain and endurance that I needed seemed unfair.

Days went by, even weeks, where I would stop and think, *Yes, I've lost my job because I was injured.* I counted over 15,000 patients that I had cared for during the course of my nursing career. Now it was my turn to be cared for but all was different from what it seemed.

I had heard about the injustice of the system but until you are affected you can never really believe it will happen to you. I sunk into depression but, more than anything, I began to see people for who they really were.

It was a disaster.

The road

The WorkCover case dragged on and on. For years, in fact. The injury changed the course of my life – it was the fork in the road, the twist and turn of fate. I had never really been one to stand my ground, and instead went with the flow of things. This could have been reflected in my music and art work. For me, to speak up was difficult; I had to learn that. I was deemed unable to return to the type of nursing that I had been doing and so a change was in the wind. It was a turning point. I realised the time had come to say goodbye to the woman who was and say hello to the new. That became a turning point fuelled by loss.

I recognised what I call 'the soul of care', which is fertile and gives growth. When we merge in the space of 'the other', we merge with consciousness of a type, we merge with the divine and in part play an important and mighty role in healing. This is the joy of making well and setting the suffering free if possible with 'the soul of care'. As I reflected back on my nursing, I recognised I was present in palliative care with families and patients.

There were days when I questioned the road I was on. What was the point of it all? What relevance did the psychic and mediumistic experiences have, what deeper meaning did they bring when the chips were down? Days of not having enough to survive on and barely making it through. I would transfer $1 on my iphone just for the hell of it. Laughing at the insanity of it all. Constantly hoping and praying for resolution. It felt vacuous, as if I were in suspended animation. Studying philosophy actually helped find a deeper meaning in the suffering. Having a future plan to live for helped in the survival. I had to fight. To turn around and give up on everything I believed in wasn't part of the fabric of my soul. I gave it to God. I decided to break it all down to a cellular level. Drop the facade and go out into the sunlight just as I was, broken. I accepted the delays and worked with that canvas. I witnessed the smugness on the faces of many during the dark days, when I mentioned I was a medium, when going without, when I was hungry, eating what I had rather than what I wanted to eat or simply a biscuit. I wondered what my story would bring to the universe I was existing in. Were there those here who were a bridge for the other side to communicate through? Light kept breaking in, the planet kept moving, laughter was still in the air and the seasons turned as they always do.

I knew suddenly what it was like to be injured, to suffer a loss. I could read in people's faces those who cared and those who didn't. Many times I thought of the beer can that rose into the air. The force beyond. The force that opens flowers and moves the earth around the sun, the force of love.

My soul was crying but not for me, for others who could not see and who were blinded in the material world, harsh and blunt, glittery and shining or so it seemed.

You don't need an object to move into the air, we are all part of that force. I entertained the idea of writing and doing platform presentations in the spiritualist churches and public audiences. During the course of being out of work, I was able to do this.

I decided to study religion and philosophy as well to make the most of the time I was given. It proved to be so beneficial for me personally and for my work as a medium. I was given time to reflect and study 'the philosophy of life'. I was so grateful. I received a Graduate Diploma of Pastoral Care. Another dream had come true but it would not have been possible had I not injured myself.

During that time I was also called up by a friend to see if I could do some public platform demonstrations. They went very well and during one of them, a reverend of one of the Spiritualist Churches in Melbourne witnessed the work and later called on me to demonstrate at her church and then to run a psychic circle.

It was life-changing to say the least. They say the Lord works in mysterious ways and, I have to say, I very much believe this to be true. During the time that I was out of work I tried to make the most of things.

Recognising the financial stress, I called upon what I had been given spiritually and could see that if I were grateful about the change of circumstances, I might survive. In fact, I was able to see things then that I couldn't before. By the end of that phase I was exhausted physically, emotionally and financially. I had pretty much collapsed, desperate for help. Friends assisted and loaned me money to survive. I moved out of where I was living because I couldn't afford it and sold my car to pay the rent. It was a disaster but I kept on striving to keep going forward. My mediumistic platform demonstrations didn't suffer but I knew eventually I would fall in a heap.

If my soul wanted to grow stronger, and choose a scenario in which it could, it certainly did so. In time, I was able to see more about the situation than just the situation – I was able to see more clearly my soul, my path. I had to reveal during that time that I was a psychic medium as I was doing readings and that was a journey in itself. I had previously preferred to keep it to myself as I was aware of the repercussions and biases that would follow. I was lucky enough to have an amazing team as back-up and some who also had had experiences of their own and consequently weren't judgemental.

It all fell together piece by piece, word by word, day by day until the saga ended.

My heart was broken and at times my faith was tested. The chronic pain went on and on, and the situation seemed never-ending, fighting for the side that was injured and the loss of my job. There were times I just lost it, consumed by the situation and overwhelmed.

There were days with very little food and no money at all. I would put five dollars of petrol in the car and hope for the best. I pawned rings, iPads along with selling my car to get by. I was constantly in debt, hounded for what I owed. My neighbours were great, and although they weren't privy to the whole story, they loaned me butter, milk and coffee and made me laugh. When my grandson was born, I couldn't buy him anything to welcome him into the world. It was weeks before I bought him two T-shirts.

It was then that I recognised the hurt and saw that it was not only me experiencing an injustice but also my daughter, her partner and my grandson who had lost out as well. That was when it really got to me and that was when I felt God, the Creator, the Great Spirit, speak and surround me with the eternal love of the universe that is present for us all. I began to own it, all the injustice, discrepancies and total disruption of my soul. It belonged to me and I was going to face it head-on and bring in the universe as well.

New friends emerged that listened and 'got it'. They were true and loyal and had my back. Their words healed my broken heart and restored the faith that I had lost in humanity. I saw human nature. I saw evil, fake smiles and unsympathetic gestures and words. I almost felt stripped of my humanity at times.

By the time I got to a placement for pastoral care study I was a nervous wreck, but got through. I was so lucky to have such an understanding team who fully supported the position I was in and showed me so much empathy and compassion. I felt safe and nurtured in that environment.

I started to feel my own energy more at this point in time. I began to re-identify again. I began to see more into the hearts of others and was able to read them without them even being aware.

At one point I remember I awoke in the middle of the night and thanked God for letting me suffer the way I had. You may now ask why, and it may seem as if I'm sounding like a hypocrite. It was in the depths of despair and desolation that I saw things. A couple of friends at one stage loaned me some money, a small amount but life-saving. I can't put into words how grateful I was to have that assistance – between them and a sister I was able to get on my feet.

I expect I felt like a lot of people do who suffer a type of trauma and it feels as if the world is revolving and moving while somehow you just feel numb. Like being on a train and knowing where you want to get off but being unable to move past the crowd in the train to actually alight. There were times I could feel my soul lift in and out of my body with all of its pain and life lessons. I coached it back within to reside and stay, knowing there was more to learn, grateful I had seen what I didn't want to see, grateful that I had learned more than I could have imagined.

Mentor

My mentor Jill had said when she passed over she would keep an eye on us. During the time I was injured I had quite a significant dream.

I dreamt I was in New Zealand, somewhere I have always wanted to visit, and I had met a new guy. He said his name was Jill in my dream.

I said, 'Oh, you mean your name is Gill.'

He replied quite gently and firmly that his name was Jill.

I remember thinking that was quite odd but the dream continued. In the next part of my dream, this guy named Jill had pulled out a gun and was shooting at a church that was standing in the middle of a grassy paddock. It was an old but beautiful church and in my dream I was petrified, stunned, shocked and so disappointed that he would do such a thing.

Then I awoke suddenly.

It took a moment to recoil out of the shock but after a minute or so thinking that it was really weird that the guy in my dream had the name Jill it suddenly occurred to me that Jill was my mentor from over 25 years prior and she was giving me a message.

I was the church that was being shot down and so I should stay strong and dignified; a church is a place of worship and honourable, and I should envelop these qualities.

She was also showing me that I would be hurt and attacked by the 'powers that be' during this intense period of my life, as I was.

During that period there were many moments of disillusionment, pain, bullying and deception.

I believe she and the spirit world were watching over me and giving me a message to stay strong and be brave. I did.

Whether it was my mentor or not and Spirit used her name through my subconscious, Spirit will try their best to come through, and dreams are a wonderful way for them to communicate as the conscious mind is rested and we can absorb information without the day-to-day conscious mind trying to analyse it in a more clinical fashion. I was psychically tapping in as well. Whichever way you would like to interpret it, I received insight.

The dream where I dreamt I would be attacked by the powers over the case was playing out. The premonition was correct, the dream was right and the warning from my mentor on the other side was accurate and taken on board. I maintained my nobility and struggled with determination and tenacity.

The Lord works in mysterious ways. Having faith in a power that is above and beyond our control, I started to again believe that things would work out according to God's plan. So I wrote and did readings, continued to do platform mediumship presentations at the spiritual churches and developed a learning manual in psychic mediumship. I gave the suffering to God. I met the people who believed in me and wove the tapestry that today is a new life.

I prayed and began listening to and composing music again. I saw a light within and found my heart, which guided me back. Although it had been broken and shattered, I picked up the pieces and was able to look people in the eye and say, 'I'm a medium and I speak to spirits. I dance with them, I sing to them, I trust in my heart and soul. They know me, this spirit world, and they love me for who I am, they hear me, the soul that is. I will enjoy the time that I have left in this body and as a soul will nurse those still on this side and through the other in love.'

Divine plan

Marion was a family friend.

We got talking one day as I was cleaning up her house. She asked me if I wanted to know why she started smoking. I didn't know what to say at first but I said, 'Um, sure.'

She said the day she started smoking was the day that the police came to her door and told her that she had lost a son in a car accident.

My heart sank to the ground. I just wanted to kneel next to her. We all loved Marion and not a thing was ever too much to do for her. Many times since she has passed I have thought of her. I know she resides in heaven with the angels and would have been greeted by the tender loving caress of her boy.

She and I spoke of spiritual things. I remember once saying to her, 'Is there someone up there whose name starts with H?'

'Yes, that's Harry, my husband who passed.'

'And an M?'

'Yes, that's Michael.'

'And Marion, is there a small dog as well?'

'Yes, there is.'

And she proceeded to say that after the little dog had passed, she would often hear his voice. Similar to Elsie and her dog Beau, Marion would especially hear her dog before she would have a shower as the dog would always follow her to the bathroom just beforehand.

During the episode of the injury that I had at work, I woke up one morning after dreaming that Marion had visited me to see if I was okay. The care and love as a friend looking after her had been remembered as she crept in on me on the earthly plane to see how I was doing. The suffering and loss that she had experienced while here on Earth was unbearable but love has no boundaries – the smiles, the care, the sincerity, the friendships surmount to more than gold and empires. The love we give unconditionally returns. If there ever was an angel on the earth it would have been Marion. For ever and ever she lives in my heart and I'm so happy she is now reunited with her boy in heaven. On the higher planes up there she can now rest and travel back to earth on her frequent angel pass.

Months later while waiting on a hearing regarding my case, I put on Elton John in the car and the song that came on was 'Candle in the Wind' from the church service of Princess Diana's funeral. He sounded so amazing singing, so raw, so pure, full of emotion and honesty, humility and grace. Those sounds were what I needed and I remembered the time that I had seen the black crosses on people the week before her death.

I changed lanes as I was driving along thinking of this and the WorkCover nightmare that I was enduring. It seemed as if time had stopped still as I noticed the car in front of me bore the number plate D1ANA. I couldn't believe my eyes, and as I write this it still feels unreal. The name Diana on the number plate in front of me as the song of the funeral was playing in my car. The universe was playing synchronicity. Good people get hurt sometimes.

I took comfort then and there that I was a part of a series of events that were playing out. I had faith again, although at the time I was still unsure of the outcome.

But I had faith. I wasn't giving up. I took it as a sign that Spirit had my back.

I thought for a moment and then felt I had learnt about love and fear, I had learnt who my true friends were, the ones who cared, I had learnt about integrity, honesty, truth, honour, bravery, humility, patience, kindness, forgiveness, deception, karma and faith.

I had learnt all of that through an injury one night at work. I had suddenly seen grace in some faces and those who had taken the time out to see how I was doing.

Psychic children

Children are so sensitive and untainted by the materialistic world that we live in, and can be open to the world of spirit naturally. Children will do and say things at times without the filtering of adults, some even recall past lifetimes and can bring through such knowledge and gifts.

Justine had arrived for a reading and as we proceeded I could sense the feeling of a father in the spirit world who had not long passed. This was confirmed and he had passed over from cancer only months before she came to see me.

Justine had two children; Harry was six years old and Emily was younger. Justine's father had been diagnosed with prostate cancer that had metastasised to the colon. He had rapidly deteriorated over a period of months. It became too difficult to look after him at home and, because of his deterioration, he was moved into palliative care for the remainder of his days. The family took it in turns to see him. Justine would take Harry and Emily along to see their grandfather before his time to pass came.

He was well medicated and out of pain, his pupils the size of pin pricks as he lay almost motionless, topped up with a syringe driver filled with morphine. He would smile when he saw his grandchildren and at the delight they had given him. He held Justine's hand as Harry quietly took in the atmosphere. The palliative care house had a piano and the pastoral care worker there played 'Moon River', her father George's favourite song one afternoon as the family vigilantly awaited the inevitable.

Justine remembered it was a Monday night and she had put Harry to bed after bath time as usual with a Hans Christian Anderson fairytale that he dearly loved to hear. He was tired and fell asleep.

It was 11.45pm when Justine heard Harry crying and she went into his room. He was sitting up awake in bed when she came into the room.

He said, 'Mum, Grandpa has gone to sleep forever.'

She just cried when she heard him say this. She replied, 'Harry, it's okay, we will see Grandpa today.'

The doctors from palliative care had actually assured the family that George still had time and that the end, although near, was not immediately imminent.

Then Harry said again, 'Mummy, Grandpa has gone to sleep forever.'

Justine settled Harry down. 'Yes, honey, Grandpa is not well but he is still with us and I will take you to see him in the morning.'

She tucked the blankets in and stroked his head as he quietly drifted off into slumberland. Fifteen minutes later the phone rang, and it was Justine's mother.

'Darling,' she said, 'we just got the call. Your father has passed away.'

There are stories of children picking up on relatives who have passed or knowing of a specific time or day that they pass when no knowledge of their illness was spoken about to the child prior. Many young children can see and talk to relatives who have passed and may pass on information that they could not possibly have known, like Grandma liked playing the piano, when they were never told that their grandmother even knew how to play piano. Just like in Justine's story, our little ones appear to have heavenly radars and a natural sixth sense, if only we would listen.

Eight months before my daughter fell pregnant, my mother, sister and myself all dreamt of a baby coming for her within a two-week period. Interesting that the soul of this baby was making its impact well before it was due to arrive in the world through a dream. She had been praying for a baby. Her prayer was answered.

In my dream, I saw my grandmother knitting and then I saw my sister who had passed with a baby wrapped in a blue cloth as she was nursing the child in the spirit world. The dream needed no complex interpretation, it was clear to me a baby was coming for my daughter. How precious the soul, and how precious life and the journey we share. Intertwined and sacred as we travel along a path. She did, in fact, give birth to a beautiful baby boy.

Ego and the medium

As part of my quest to investigate psychic phenomena and mediumship and as part of my life journey, I decided to study pastoral care at university. After the injury, I thought it would be a good mixture, marrying theology, philosophy and religion to further understand what was happening mediumistically.

Part of the course was a subject on our inner lives as a disciple, and I gleaned much from taking this subject. We also had to look at the ego to see where it might fit in to our daily existence and how it affected our psyche. As a medium, the ego can sometimes get in the way of development, saying 'you can't do this or that'. Eager to delve more into the psychology, I found David Benners' writing from *The gift of being yourself* helpful in releasing some of the myths and confusion I had perceived. The following information is what I gathered.

I've learned that the ego-self I have collected along the way in my journey of life could hold me back. It could stunt my growth and disable me, if I became disillusioned because of it. I cannot be any closer to Source or God if I continue along the path of the ego and I need to let go of it. Surrender it and thank it for showing me the traps and illusions that it brings to my awareness. It no longer serves my higher purpose and that is to be more fully with Source or God in His presence and understanding.

There is a transformation and a blessing when I release the ego and I can see myself as I truly am and I can accept myself for who I truly am. For He made me, I am not of my own making. I belong with the universe as much as I am here on the earth in the physical. I am also part of the cosmos.

When I let go of the ego, I can then overcome previous pains and wounds that I have collected in my life or see them from another perspective and how they may have affected and created the ego. Like shedding a skin, I can be closer to the core of my soul, who I really am. I have new colours to explore and new healings that surface for me.

I needed to let go of the outer layer, which was protecting the insecurities, mistrust, shame, guilt and shortcomings that were holding me at bay, where I was unable to express and more fully sympathise and realise the Creator's full love. In the shadow of the ego, I lay asleep and content in my own disillusion until I could wake up and see myself for who I really am, a child of God, more filled with love and ready to do His work.

The problem with having false ways and attachments is that it creates the false self. When we displace God/The All/Creator, we become 'The All' within our self as we become a false self. The value of our 'self' becomes glued to the attachments we find value in, be it material possessions or the way we look or our career which defines us. We move away from the Creator, the divine, and begin to undiscover the glory. We put value into questions pertaining to 'what I have', 'what others think of me'. The false self is an easy trap to fall into and I see it every day in the media and in people – a shallow grating of the human experience and it saddens me. It saddens me to see my own conditional value systems as well but I can be mindful of them by turning my direction and orientation to something sacred.

By keeping these attachments as valuable possessions, I mask my true identity as I assume that I know better than God, the Source, the universal power, and in that way I'm not really listening to God. I've misconstrued my real identity by having these attachments and cheated myself because of insecurities; I've lost myself. I can only find myself again through the Creator, Source, God – He is the beginning and the end so I should then start at the beginning again.

Ego isn't my enemy but can be like a child that is demanding and insecure, even bossy because it can hurt. If I can notice it and listen to its demands, I can lovingly reassure it that it should listen to the soul, a greater authority. Then I believe I have the right balance.

Every day, it's important to have the discipline and mindset that we are spirits in a physical form. We are here for a limited time only in this body and are destined to return back to Source when our time is nigh. Every day is a miracle and a chance to commune and give back.

Humility is the key to remember – do not forget our existence is miraculous.

'We are not God. We are not our own origin, nor are we our own ultimate fulfillment. To claim to be so is a suicidal act that wounds our faith relationship with the living God and replaces it with a futile faith in a self that can never exist.'[4]

---

4 Benner, D. G, *The gift of being yourself: The spiritual journey*, Illinois, InterVarsity Press, 2015, p. 73

Frequently asked questions

Can you see for yourself?

Yes, but the expectation to see for myself is less intense now than it used to be. I believe that spirits are looking after us and will show or present to us in ways that are intended to help. Not that long ago, I went through a very intense WorkCover experience. I was injured while on night duty at a major hospital. My right shoulder was operated on – they found a tear. There were complications with my neck post-surgery and I indured numbness to my hands.

It was awful and it dragged on and on. During this time, I wrote about doing a meditation and seeing my grandfather and my sister showing me scissors and cutting through material, which I interpreted as having to have surgery before they announced that I would.

It's important to be mindful not to rely on seeing for ourselves as opposed to making certain decisions with our rational and logical mind as well. We shouldn't be so naïve as to rely on an outside force to be always making decisions for us; that takes away our power and choices that we have. Life on earth is miraculous.

How do you prepare for this type of work? Are you clairaudient, clairvoyant or clairsentient?

Yes, all three. I can hear, feel and see spirits. Hopefully that gets the correct message through to the recipient in the earthly world. I prepare with prayer and meditation, and practise this diligently through the week. I try to be respectful, walk the walk and to keep developing.

Sometimes when I'm out I may sense that a spirit wishes to make contact with someone but it's inappropriate to simply pull someone aside and say 'excuse me, your uncle is here with us'. There's a time and a place to commune. It's sacred.

Hearing it in my mind is different from when you're saying something to yourself. For me, it's a different sound coming from a different place and I know that's spirit talk.

Are mediums open all the time?

It is possible to be open a lot of the time but it's healthier to shut down and rest. As an example, I was out at a party with a friend and met a guy. While talking to him, I kept feeling that I had a really sore throat. As the conversation developed, I asked him if he had ever had a problem with his throat as mine felt scratchy standing next to him. He told me that he had swallowed a small coin as a child, was operated on to remove it and it left scar tissue in his throat.

I believe these days I'm better at switching off and leading a more balanced life, but when I was developing I used to absorb things and get swamped.

Protection – what's that all about?

There seems to be two schools of thought here. One is that connecting to the world of spirit is a natural occurrence and that the 'spirit world look after their own'. So there's no need to do the protection rituals. I've taken both ideas on board. Not getting stuck in rituals and opening and closing the chakra energy centres. The other theory is that just like there are good and bad people on the earthly plane, there are good and bad in the spirit realm. Many psychics and mediums will burn incense or sage to clear areas in rooms and houses or sprinkle them with salt. They might even do meditation and cover themselves in a 'white light'. Or protect themselves by imagining they are sitting in a bubble of protection. In psychic work we can be affected by negative energy from others and even locations and so it's a good idea to be mindful that we are more than the physical, and the energetic body around us can be an interpreter. Being aware can elicit insight and by having the insight that we are a soul whose energy is sensitive, we can be more mindful. Personally I like prayer and being mindful of the fact that I'm a soul that needs nourishing. I also find meditation healing.

Residual energy is where ghostly phenomena have been explained as an energy imprint rather than 'a ghost trapped in a building that needs rescuing'. When a spirit passes they are immediately in the light. The many sightings and feelings that people have are a build-up of residual energy that a building or area can contain. Places like older historic buildings and ancient sites can have an energetic resonance about them. This energy has been built by real souls and real stories through the ages and can leave an imprint of energy. Sensitive people can pick up on this and read it. Like walking through a building you've never been to before and sensing things like events, names, stories connected to who might have lived there or stayed in the premises or locations. A sensitive could pick up on an energy imprinted in a house or location visually by feeling or even hearing, almost like reliving an occurrence that has already happened. It doesn't mean there's a ghost there or that we can be harmed. I'm not discounting the amazing stories that have been gifted through sightings and visitations that are incredible all through the ages and all over the world. Stories that are precious and help us further understand how the two worlds unite.

We had taken Mum out for her 85th birthday to an old historic building in Melbourne that catered for events, and we chose the high tea. We gathered as sisters at the venue, which was built in the early 1900s with intricate leadlight and plasterwork throughout. It was decorated in a traditional style and upon entering I felt as if I were transferred back to another era. From the 1930s, it was opened full-time for functions. We were aware that it had housed orphans, and soldiers had stayed there during the war years as well.

The lady who served us was middle-aged and diligent in her manner, smiling and laughing with us as she put down sandwiches, cakes and scones. We got talking to her and when one of my sisters asked her to tell us about the place, she was quite open.

'Oh, I heard voices here after work one night. No one else was here and I was closing up and I heard a voice say, "What are you doing?" It wasn't the first time and it came from the kitchen area.'

Our jaws dropped as she spoke the words but at the same time I understood the concept of residual energy and how that might play out. It was fascinating to hear the story and it just goes to show that energy imprints do really occur.

As we connect to the spirit world we should be responsible for our safety. Mediums are working between the two worlds as a conduit, a bridge, but we can disconnect at any time by saying in our minds, 'I wish to disconnect now' or 'I'm shutting down now'. It is important to keep a healthy balance for the mind, body and spirit. Some even say they have seen people reside in these places as well.

When I first joined a circle we opened the chakra centres to commune with spirit and closed them with good intention when finished. You will notice with many of my experiences they just happened naturally without any sort of procedure prior. I open with the best intentions, being mindful that I'm about to commune with spirit and that there is that liminal space where I shift my consciousness and when finished close gracefully, thanking those spirits who come forward and work with me and I say a prayer. I'm attuned to working both ways. It's not just when I'm reading for someone or doing a platform mediumship demonstration; I also strive to be spiritual in my life and that informs my life and the learning and training that I have gathered. I also liken the idea of mediumistic work in caring for oneself with some of the caring professions such as counselling, where the energy of the 'other' in a session is taken on. The idea of being able to download is important, as well as a debrief with a spiritual supervisor; this is necessary at times. I keep an open mind that there is always much more to learn and as mediums in the world share their own personal stories, perhaps we will glean and understand more.

Do you believe that the world is becoming more spiritual?

I hope so. I believe I'm one of millions around the world who are psychic mediums, developed and undeveloped, receiving messages and signals and giving and passing on the information. Many of us are demonstrating and putting it out there, showing that we are part of the realm that isn't disconnected to the afterlife so the world grows and consciousness expands.

Friends and colleagues I've worked with also have many stories that have helped to give them insight into life beyond this life.

As technology grows and the internet gives us as human beings the ability to see and be connected to each other, so too with mediums. We are coming together as it's easier now with the internet to create a world wide web of spirit knowledge for the next generation to glean from. With so many people coming forward now and giving 'proof of survival' with verified evidence through platform mediumship, it's difficult to just sweep it under the carpet and pretend it doesn't exist.

Spiritualism opens a door to humanity; that there is a Source, a God, a great spirit that is all-seeing and all-knowing. We can all exist as one in peace and harmony for the greater good.

It appears that people are more open-minded these days and acknowledge that there is more to learn.

I'd read just recently that someone wrote 'speaking to the dead' and I understood what they meant but thought to myself, the soul doesn't die. I believe that as we search for deeper meanings we as a collective can be inspired by all religions and mystics from the dawn of time. Soul education the big questions like 'Where do we come from' and 'where are we going beyond this life' are queries that will always be ever present in a society. Being more spiritually enriched in my perspective is also about being sensitive to the needs of my fellow man. We are all children of the universe and it's not about material possessions. Nature can teach and inspire us to listen more deeply. Coming from a heart centred space without judgement in peace will always be golden no matter where we are. If we think of it as already being spiritual and knowing that we are here for a time with loved ones can gift us with the recognition of our soul travelling through time and space for it has a finite time here to journey and explore new regions and boundaries that we are born to. Our healers in all fields our teachers, scientists and hard labourer's are equally equipped with the vision to understand what it means to be intuitive and heartfelt. Suffering can bring deeper knowledge within because we see with fresh eyes beyond the physical we see through where we are and more into the heart. Mankind may venture out into space or create the most incredible cures and temples but it is the temple within that will always be most precious as it is bound to return back to source. We are time itself perhaps and as such know.

As Maya Angelou says, we can be rainbows in other people's clouds:

> 'Prepare yourself so that you can be a rainbow in somebody else's cloud; somebody that may not look like you, may not call God the same name that you call God, if they call God at all, you see? And may not eat the same dishes prepared the way you do, may not dance your dances, or speak your language. But, be a blessing to somebody. That's what I think.'[5]

Is there a difference between a psychic and a medium?

Yes, there is a difference – the psychic doesn't connect with the spirit world, so does not receive information from spirits. A psychic will use the 'clair senses', clairvoyance, clairaudience, clairsentience and claircognisance, to tune in to the auric field and to read the past, present and future possibilities, whereas a medium will use those 'clairs' to connect in with the spirit world. *Not all psychics are mediums but all mediums are psychic.*

Everyone is psychic to some degree – the next level up from intuition. A psychic can tune into the energy of a person, a place or even an object, sensing the energy of past, present and future. A medium also uses their superconscious and subconscious mind – if we were using our conscious mind to interpret information, it would be too rational as we need to go deeper. A medium needs a strong basis of psychic ability as they become a conduit between the spirit world and the physical world that we reside in. The spirit world vibrates at a higher frequency, a quicker frequency and the world of the physical vibrates at a slower frequency. The medium is the link connecting the two worlds, and can pass on information that they receive.

---

5   Maya Angelou, www.openhorizons.org/four-ideas-to-live-by-the-interfaith-theopoetics-of-maya-angelou.

How important is prayer?

According to David Benner, 'Prayer is the soul's native language; as natural as breathing'.[6] I'm praying that my heart stays open and I'm praying for love and kindness. I'm praying for those who are sick and frail, the brotherhood of man and peace on earth. I pray knowing that I'm part of the Creator's sacred universe and one of his children, like all of us.

I'm praying for wisdom, insight, forgiveness, understanding. I'm praying for the human race and that we can embody unconditional love and understanding between each other. I'm praying for Mother Earth and her survival. I'm praying that the heart of my soul survives this life as I take with me eternally all the knowledge that I've contained within and those that I've loved. This is like the bread of life that enriches my relationship as I breath it into my soul. I'm praying with a candle lit in the presence of the Lord and my heart knows the words that fall from my soul and land on God's carpet, woven into his love and care.

When we pray before and after opening to Spirit, it gives a reverence to our work. It brings in the sacred and prepares us for something that is divine. It assists in setting the intention for working with Spirit for the highest good. Spirits are aware of this as well and vibrate towards those who operate with loving intentions.

How many types of mediumship are there?

There are two types of mediumship and the first is mental mediumship, meaning through the mind. This is telepathy in that communication is transferred from the spirit world to the medium through thoughts that are picked up by the medium and interpreted to the sitter or audience. The conversation from the spirit world is facilitated from mind to mind or consciousness to consciousness through telepathy. As mediums we use our 'clair' abilities to perceive what the messages are. We blend our minds with spirit discarnate.

The other type of mediumship is called physical mediumship, and

---

6 Benner, D. G, *Opening to God*, Illinois, InterVarsity Press, 2010, p. 15

there are various kinds. This type can be witnessed by more than one person so therefore provides proof of survival in the afterlife. In trance mediumship the spirit world can manipulate the energies of a medium and can materialise from the spirit world to ours. There are differing types of physical mediumship and in trance it is powered by others sitting for a medium. Physical mediumship is done in a darkened room with a red light, though blue can be used as well, as lecturer Martin Twycross explained to me. Things that can occur are direct voice materialisations, apports, transfiguration, aromas, levitations, raps, knocks and people feeling touches from the spirit realm. With transfiguration, the face of a loved one builds up and likenesses have been seen to be remarkable. With direct voice phenomena, a voice can be heard through an artificial voice box.

Apports have been seen to appear in these circumstances and have been materialised by spirit. Objects can disappear and be transported to other areas. Objects that have been apported are things such as coins, jewellery, books and other items pertinent to the one experiencing the phenomena. In my experience, it was my alarm clock that was near my bed that ended up in the bathroom weeks before my father died. Levitation has been known to occur, especially with table tipping where tables have been seen to elevate into the air. Raps and knocks are also another physical mediumship phenomena. Orbs and lights are another that can appear as well. My mother stated that after my sister passed she noticed a blue light emanating from the ceiling that was quite prominent. She felt that it was in connection to her soul.

What is a development circle?

A development circle is held under the guidance of an experienced medium as a training forum for developing mediumship. With the discipline of meditation and visualisation, the development of clairvoyance, clairaudience, clairsentience and claircognisance may be exercised within a group. Within a circle, spirit people are asked to draw near and experiences such as psychic breezes, where coldness may be experienced over part or all of the body, may be felt. These circles should be run by those who are experienced in the field of mediumship. Coming into contact with your guides and doing short readings for others are part of circle development.

When I was sitting in my original psychic circle over 25 years ago, all six of us present could smell lemons in the air. It was amazing that we could all smell it at the same time and it was proof of the mystical ways that spirits work with us here on earth. Impressions within the mind of pictures, words, thoughts and even smells may be received.

The unfoldment of mediumship is a lifelong process and learning never ceases. Along with the learning comes the grace and respect needed to deliver the message and be a competent link between two worlds. With mediumship comes a responsibility and it is recommended by spiritualists that a student studying mediumship also study philosophy of spiritualism and look into the teachings of the great philosophers to gain a deeper understanding of life, mortality and the world beyond this one.

Can anyone become a medium?

There seems to be two angles to this question – some say you are born a medium and that it is in the DNA, while others say that it can be developed. I liken it to this. Yes, we can all develop psychically and mediumistically and learn to be more open to the world of spirit. Some will be more so and others less. Psychic/mediumistic gifts can be present from a young age, especially in children who are less tainted by the world and more innocent. They may talk about seeing and hearing Uncle Ted say goodbye and that he is okay on the night he passed.

Sometimes psychic gifts can emerge quite suddenly and the recipient can go on to do some amazing work after such instances as a near death experience where they travel outside of the physical body and see themselves lying on an operating table. From that point on, because of the spiritual experience of sensing their own spiritual body, they are able to emerge into the realms of the spiritual psychic without the bias of those who have not experienced such a spiritual encounter for themselves. Or it may be in the case of losing a loved one and hearing or seeing their spirit that triggers the antenna to a mediumistic connection.

It will be unique for each individual and, as long as the intention is pure, the spirit world will continue to work with that individual. I have seen that it is indeed carried on in the ancestral line but that it is also up to the individual to enhance and develop the natural abilities gifted.

Can we bring through who the sitter wants?

A lot of times clients will present and want to speak with a specific loved one, and that's fair enough. The question is, though, can we bring them through? If we think of mediumship as a radio wave, working on different frequencies, some spirits are easier to access according to the particular energy or frequency of the medium. Some mediums can work with a wider and more powerful range of energy and some have a smaller range. Also, the spirit world may not wish to work through some mediums because they don't resonate with a particular medium's wavelength. It is thought that when we travel back to the spirit world, we need to learn how to communicate through a medium just as a medium on the earthly plane learns how to communicate with the spirit world. Just like here on earth, some souls are able to communicate more easily than others. Bringing through the soul of the spirit of a loved one is the ultimate in a reading and can bring such healing and love and proof of survival, but the conditions need to be right. Sometimes it just isn't the right time and the spirit world is wise beyond our knowing; time there is different from time here on the earthly plane. Spirits on that side have free will, too. It can't be forced and it shouldn't be forced. I prefer to hand it over to the Creator.

Sometimes, too, in a reading, whether it be a one to one or on platform, there is an 'enabling communicator' who helps to set up the conditions to be more conducive for the spirit that the sitter really wishes to communicate with. If the sitter has lost a child, sometimes it may be the grandfather who comes through first with love and beautiful words to set the path for the child to come through and speak, knowing that it will be easier for the sitter to take the messages in and sit with the reading in a more comfortable way. Spirit knows and it's always a good idea to be sensitive and listen with the heart.

If the parting has been sudden and traumatic, a period of adjustment may be needed for both parties. Spirit will quite often bring through what we need as opposed to what we want.

What are double links?

During platform mediumship we can do double links and it is fascinating that two mediums can link into a soul and receive information from the same soul. It is true even if the mediums are in the same room or even country. Think of it like a family where members may be at opposite ends of the world but still hear or see a message from the same soul at the same time about the same subject matter. Mediums quite often will receive messages from a spirit even before a sitter arrives for a reading and even before doing a platform demonstration. The idea is to be in the moment and relay what is given by the spirit, but the spirit world is a consciousness and intelligence of its own and sometimes if the message is important it will be relayed from Spirit prior, as in the young boy in spirit who came to me the day before the platform presentation. This spirit wanted to make sure that he was mentioned to his parents. The power of love prevails. Spirit had the bigger picture in mind. I've learned to live this way now.

Where does the soul travel?

While I was being mentored, there was talk and speculation of how the soul travelled once beyond this life. Of course, the topic is as old as time immemorial. We used to read photographs and someone in my circle told me that my grandmother was nursing on the other side. It was something that resonated with me because she had two cousins who were paediatric physicians and surgeons and she was quite the healer herself in her own womanly wise way as I remember growing up. She had a knack when we were unwell as children with knowing what to do and how to care for myself and my sisters.

There are some who question as to whether the spirit world can see those who they have loved on this earth and what they might be doing once the earthly journey here has ceased. I can say that from doing platform mediumship, many souls have tried their hardest to come through and let their loved ones know that they are aware of what's happening to them and things they may have been experiencing such as hardship, job loss, an illness in the family or even birthdays. They are aware of names, events and other things specific, such as 'the birthday cake was crushed at the birthday party and you were wearing a blue dress' — what we call evidence to reveal that there is consciousness beyond this realm.

It was June of 2018 and I had a dream. It seemed as if someone had been in a fire — so much so that I was feeling as if it were me. I saw two people and I knew even though I was dreaming that there was a veil but I could see beyond it. There were doors of some sort that almost looked like the ones we have here in a hospital and there was a group of people. I heard them say, 'We have another one.' I could see a body and a face that looked exhausted and a feeling that the soul of the person hadn't realised that they had died. They were being escorted, it seemed, by people on the other side. A healing team of souls were aware of what had happened and were kind of resuscitating the soul in a way that was accustomising them to the new realm. Then I awoke. I recognised it as a psychic dream but I didn't dwell on it.

Later that day I heard on the news that a man had passed away in the northwest of Melbourne from a house fire. Large amounts of smoke were coming from the house when the fire brigade arrived and the first crews on the scene had found a bedroom on fire. A man was trapped inside and he had died at the scene.

The story gripped me and of course I thought of the dream that I'd had that night. It opened my thoughts to the sense of wonder and miracle of life and the soul's journey and how we are healed not only on this side but on the other as well. The thought of being met by a team on the other side as we cross was comforting.

They say we choose the lessons we need to evolve as a soul and that we choose our family as a team that our soul can evolve through and teach and learn.

How will demonstrating empathy help you in your communication?

Demonstrating empathy is crucial in psychic mediumistic work as it fosters a deeper link for communicating. It can assist with helping clients as well to open up and feel comfortable should they wish to reveal more about their life journey. Recent research has shown this. Dr Helen Reiss in her 'Power of Empathy'[7] talk demonstrates through an experiment with a recipient of counselling – she and her counsellor were monitored with physiological tracers that compared heart rates. The insightful monitoring revealed by a graph showed that when the heart rate was elevated in the recipient it was also matched and elevated in the counsellor at the same time, showing an empathic wave of relative concern. This may have been demonstrated through behaviour such as a gesture or a grimace from the counsellor. It may have been through soft body language, and a sincere tone of voice. It may have been through the timing and wording of empathic questions as opposed to sentences that revealed a nonchalant attitude. Empathic listening can also be constructive and gain a sense of relationship that will enhance the quality and outcome of resolutions and possible referral needs of the client. It builds trust. Professional boundaries need to be in place but empathy is a foundation to build a great rapport for a good counsellor/client relationship.

Having empathy from the outset helps to bond during psychic and mediumistic work. Being an empathic person and caring for the other is like being a good samaritan. Empathy is especially noted in clairsentient work; it's that gut feeling where we might know something doesn't feel right. As a medium, empathy helps me distinguish messages, and to know if I'm getting it right for the recipient. I always check in through empathy as it's the key to being truly present, letting go of any thoughts or worries that I might be bringing to the table, and decluttering my mind and heart.

I had been invited one afternoon to a mediumship demonstration, things were going well and the medium was able to place the messages accurately but what stood out for me on this occasion was the fact that the medium was crying quite heavily at one point. Her empathy was brilliant and moving but because of the crying it got in the way of the message. I remembered early on in my development that I could be quite emotional with situations to the point where I would seem to almost take it on as if it were my issue I was dealing with in a reading. On this

---

7   Dr Helen Reiss, 'Power of empathy', www.youtube.com/watch?v=baHrcC8B4WM

particular afternoon it got to the stage where I thought someone was about to go and give the medium a glass of water to calm her down. Being so emotional can disrupt the flow of information coming through so it's important to remember that as well as having empathy; balance will assist in delivering the messages and keep the channel open. Of course at times when things are difficult to relay or upsetting there will no doubt be tears and in platform mediumship it's hard as we move from one person to the next in the congregation present at the time. We will be of more use if we can be mindful that we are switched on emotionally and there will be a load to carry during the demonstration or one to one sitting with a client but like any caring profession there is the need to be gentle with ourselves and know that the messages are coming through us as we serve the spirit world.

When the heart's in the right place, we see everything

The modalities of mediumship can be learnt and we can develop at our own pace. The world is filled today with how to learn mediumship and there is much on psychic development as well. I imagine as we move into the future there will continue to be scientific exploration of these things. We are today on the threshold of discovering more about psychic mediumship as more and more mediums are bringing forth their stories and sharing them with the world.

From what I've experienced, I have learnt that the heart and the power of love are major forces for discernment in mediumship. When my heart is in the right place, I'm able to see more and feel more. With this comes the need for self-care as well. I've seen and felt and witnessed the afterlife so I have faith and this faith makes it easier for me to connect with Spirit. I don't have to second-guess that there is no such world and so in this way I already feel connected. I strive to be the best soul I can be with all its earthly trimmings. I feel blessed for what I have witnessed and happy to share the story of my journey for others to bring hope, comfort and joy into another person's life. My motto of 'when the heart is in the right place, we see everything' is like an anchor for me. It centres and grounds my soul in the here and now.

It takes time to develop patience; the journey of life is at times like a labyrinth. If I'd known and witnessed everything too quickly, I would not have appreciated the beauty of where I'd come from. My personal struggle helped me to be free at times of the physical when I felt the presence of my own soul guiding me through. I went with my heart and trusted with faith. The heart is one of the keys to accessing the higher self, the soul.

Crossing over

It's understandable to think we are met by loved ones and family on the other side as well as our guides and master teachers who have worked and inspired us during our time on earth. These people can help us do a life review and look at the lessons our soul set out to learn, and whether we developed in the way that we wished and needed. I believe when we cross over we experience love, and we the soul have a greater understanding. You will notice throughout the book that I've mentioned seeing my sister, father and grandfather from the spirit realm. They have all made visits to me here on this side. Spiritual things have happened to me during spiritual times here on the earth; it's not something that I've willed or conjured up. During platform presentations, I've seen figures build up and give over pertinent information and had spirits come through beforehand, as they are aware that they will be able to make contact with loved ones.

I've witnessed God in this realm; for example, when the beer can elevated into the air. That speaks to me that God, the Creator, the all of our cosmic universe is part of the fabric of life. In the laugh of a child, in a frail palliated patient's eyes, in the whispering wind. For me, my religiosity is evolving. I'm open faith, I belong to all of the universe and it belongs to me. I believe I came from the One and will return there; my spiritualism tells me that my soul is eternal. I witnessed something beyond the possible when the object moved into the air as a young girl. This was like a door opening, a bridge, a connection, a sign, an unspoken language that we are more than just the physical, much more.

Didn't early cave men see apparitions and have spiritual experiences? And then these mysteries were handed down to their children's children? Didn't early men wonder about where we came from and look up at the stars and question?

According to Google, Hinduism is the oldest religion; 2000 years from now, these things may well still exist and my open faith tells me that my soul will, too.

There are countless stories the world over of people at the end of life experiencing visitations from loved ones on the other side. Stories of those in the process of leaving this side to cross over, as in a husband seeing the wife who passed before him from cancer, or an elderly mother visited by a son she lost who was stillborn. It's like a miracle in their darkest hours, knowing the grief they feel at leaving loved ones they have cared for so much. The pain and anguish of those left here knowing that soon their loved one will return home to Spirit. Yet how wonderful that those soon leaving are met by those on the other side to carry them across.

I've seen a lot of students trying to get the right message and beat themselves up if they missed something. When we are making a connection with someone who has passed, a message from someone in spirit is sacred and precious, to be cherished as a sign that the love still bonds and awakens the mystery in us all.

I witnessed the other world. I saw it, heard it, spoke up for it, reunited for it and was humbled by it. It then awakened in me love; a divine love that is greater than we can ever know. A cycle driven and deep, creative in wisdom and wonder. How could I not have been changed? For you, the reader on your quest for knowledge of the other world, know this: the love here is great, it's right where you stand, as the Creator moves through us all through the heart … the light of the heart …

A minister at my cousin's funeral said, 'Death is like boarding a ship, leaving those on one continent behind only to be greeted by those we love who are waiting for us on another shore.'

I believe when my time comes I will see her again, she will know me and we will celebrate the journey of our souls. For she has always known me, the space that separated us and the pain will be no more, she will be light and I will be lead on a path to … my butterfly sister.

For the soul can fly through the heart of another the soul has wings.

Acknowledgements

There have been many people who have influenced me throughout my life so far. They have brought with them encouragement for me to be myself, they have listened without judgement or bias and given me courage for the road ahead. The following people aren't listed in alphabetical order. The musicians I've worked with have inspired and shown me that modality is wise and angelic within itself. The nurses I've worked with have shown me humility and compassion. The chaplains have given me the gift of seeing things through the eyes of a shepherd.

With all my love I extend my thanks and gratitude …

The team at Michael Hanrahan Publishing: Michael for taking this on and his humour and kindness, Anna Clemann for all the hard work behind the scenes and dedication, Karen Comer for your wise editing, and Aisling Brady for your savvy and courage.

Lisa Hanrahan for belief and the recommendation.

Robert Handel and his printing efforts.

Shaye, for your special soul and the connection we share, thanks for keeping me on track. Let your light and love shine on those around you, my darling.

William, Harry and Abbey: thank you for being part of a new life. May we savour the journey ahead. Carmel and Peter, part of a legacy I leave. Shannon, Ben and Mia.

My sisters: Lynda, Donna, Julie and Coral. My nephews and nieces: Jonathon and Sarah, Holly, Renee, Ruby, Jack, Lucy, Heidi, Pete, Dave and Nick. Cousins Rex, Kay, Jill and Aunty Isobel and Abbey.

Rudi Katterl, Libby, Casey and Lily.

Thank you for the music and learning to just give and perform – Ulysses, Greta, Stephanie, Manny and Sarah, Peter, Belinda, Terry, George, Helen and Leon. An A-team.

Peter Kecheyes for your beautiful recordings and patience every time. Belle, Jasmine and Lochlan and your contribution.

Darren Pearce for always being there and your beautiful contribution. Yes, we are so alike, darling.

Mez, Ken, Tessa and Cassie McGregor for inspiring and teaching me about my own soul. Ken for his generous donation of his experience in the desert.

Graham and Hazel Phillimore, who picked me up every time I fell: a special note for supporting me through the darkness and holding me up through the tears.

Caroline Logan, another angel, for your support during the dark days, lifting me up, seeing light.

Ben Medhurst and sanatana house.com.au.

Meg Barry for being the truth with love.

Lauren Hall for shining the light.

Steve Kara for being the hope and for your precious encouragement every time. For the light globes during the edit and your own special psychic gifts.

Lisa Birkett for your warrior-like strength, love and loyalty, a gift to me.

Mia Johnston for your love.

Sandra Nicholls for being so compassionate and a nurse's nurse.

Heike Mitchell for your insight and love.

Omi, my soul sister.

Melissa Trent, weaving the tapestry and sorting out the threads with loving care and your precious psychic know-how.

Adriana, Annette, Kara, Amber, Amira, Daniella, Fiona, Meg, Rebecca, Melinda, Linda, Linh, Tony, Pretty, Joyce, Reuben, Pauline N and Pauline B, Clare, Coby V, Lesley, Lucy, Cely, Rose, Anna, Anthony, Marnie and Betty for your tough and thorough training. What a team! Proud to serve alongside you. Claire McGuinness for your genius and giving me the job.

Louise Bolger, Nadine Martin, Wayne Parkin, Cressida, Kim Sowter and Camille Rogers: for your encouragement, individual psychic mediumship, talent and positivity, the sharing and caring of knowledge and inspiration.

Sharon Pell for your kindness and love.

Gisella Aguirre for your wisdom and love.

Tony Tranfaglia and family.

Samantha Leslie for your angelic care.

Kylie McGregor for your support and tremendous energy. Michelle Rofique for your hard loving work.

Robert James for being there as a friend and shedding your light as a medium when you brought through Leigh. Yes, you are special.

Mystical

Cely and Joey Aldana and family for your love and care and Godlike reverence.

Sarah, Sean and Anna Jane – the early years for giving me a break.

Miche K, another angel and warrior for your ongoing love and support through the tough times. Xxx

Carol Crawford Kerr and Lorraine Le Tet for your wisdom and mediumistic teachings and Zelma as we teach and support the new.

Dee Dee for setting me straight and giving me strength to see things through and also for your psychic know-how and beautiful soul. We know what we know.

Chris Clarke, thank you for your friendship and kindness, the laughs and your precious soul. All the Clarke family are special to me. Jovan: thank you for the video and star photos, they are heavenly.

Chris Wilson, my brother in arms, what would I do without you? You saved me many times musically and world-wise.

Rob Fernandez and Karen for your kindness and generosity.

Sharon McCormack, another soul sister, for your support and guidance, for shedding light in the darkness that was. For your awesome gift as a medium. May you shine also.

Kim Greenough for always being an angel with the biggest heart.

Rennie Ozzimo and Grant for your beautiful souls.

Trevor Upton and Peter Donnelly, my other, other music family, for your inspiration and fun. You fuelled my heart.

Chevonne Fitzgerald, Craig Graham Smith, Sallyanne Hutton: harmonies from heaven and the friendships we made through music and love, an honour to sing with you.

Robyn Lester, an angel this side and wonderful medium.

Tony Stockwell and Lisa Williams for your workshops and inspiration.

Ian Breguet, Gillian Henderson and Fran Prem, mentors and most wise colleagues. Colleen Clayton, Chanh Ngyuen and Margarita Nguyen, Michelle Harley for your courage to simply be and wind the stories of the soul. My heartfelt gratitude and humility.

Jo Watling for your courage, faith and love.

Drs Mihiri, Nim and Derek.

Jill Johnson on the other side …

Esmeralda, Ron, Nana, Pa, Queenie, Bruce, Dad.

Audrey Mary Robertson.

And Leigh (my butterfly sister).

Coming soon
A guide to psychic and mediumship development book
Online course ... available through Udemy
Website: rondarobertson.com

www.ingramcontent.com/pod-product-compliance
Lightning Source LLC
Chambersburg PA
CBHW021059080526
44587CB00010B/305